RAND**THE BOOK**M
THOUGHTS

by Jack W. Smith

Library of Congress Catalog Card Number 2013914638

ISBN-13: 978-1491251454

ISBN-10: 149125145X

Published By Create Space

Printed in the USA

Dedications & Acknowledgements

This book is dedicated to my immediate and extended family who has given me many laughs and lessons and much love. My wife Vicki and my three daughters...Sarah and her husband Ted, Claire and her husband Gavin and Lauren and her husband Matt are all doing very well and are a blessing. I thank them all for their support.

Also, I would like to thank Robert and Michelle Johnson who asked me a dozen years ago to write a monthly humor column for their excellent city magazine, *The Wacoan*. It has been an extreme pleasure for me and has allowed me to create new Internet friends and share random thoughts with a great community.

Special thanks to Debbie Freeman, one of my two favorite nieces, for serving as my editor. She had done this in the past for real authors, and her expertise and advice was critical and substantial. Someone changed the rules of punctuation since I last studied English, and Debbie corrected my mistakes over and over and over and over.

Also much thanks to Polly, Robert and Lonnie of McKinleyBrown & Bradley who designed the cover and laid out the interior of this book with patience and creative excellence.

And thanks to you for reading. This book and all others.

RAND●M THE BOOK THOUGHTS

Prologue

I'm very happy to have written my third book. I didn't finish the first two.

Why did I write a book? Because I have too much time on my hands, along with ever increasing age spots. If we can send a man to the moon, why can't someone do something about old-folks-hands?

I can never say, "I know that like the back of my hand." The back of my hands look different every day depending on whether I bumped them into something getting out of bed, or waited a few minutes later. Come on scientist, do something. I know curing cancer is important, but how about our hands?

Anyway, I wrote this book because I couldn't think of anything else to do. I'd already watered the plants and taken out the garbage. Maybe I could take out the plants and water the garbage, but it wouldn't take too long, and here I'd be again.

Some or even most of this will be excerpts from the columns that I have written for *The Wacoan* for the last dozen years. *The Wacoan* is kind of like a full-fledged City Magazine for less than a full-fledged city. The column is something less than a full-fledged column. It's about half fledged. But the sad truth is that much of the world, to the potential risk of civilization, hasn't had the opportunity to read my columns. Now civilization can more easily be saved.

Most of the thoughts in the book are original, but some are no doubt stolen from years of reading what others write. Some are just plain jokes, but seem to fit. Thanks to all from whom I've stolen ideas and keep up the good work. I had a friend in high school who had a bad habit of telling the same jokes again and again. When confronted about this problem, he always said, "A good joke is good anytime". He was no rocket scientist. But then he went to college, got a degree in aeronautical engineering and worked for NASA for 30 years, where he was a rocket scientist. Who knew? Maybe a good joke is good anytime.

I have two hopes for this book. I hope that you enjoy it and I hope that you paid real cash money for it, cause my retirement plan, the lottery, hasn't worked out so far.

Disclaimer: No animals were harmed in the writing of this book, although my bad dog, Parker, was frequently bored and wanted me to leave the computer and go throw the frisbee. Parker loves for me to throw the frisbee but doesn't like to bring it back. It's a fetch-twenty-two situation.

CHAPTER ONE

Politics, Lawyers, Government

And Other Un-Natural Disasters

The federal government does a lot of really strange things. One of the most unbelievable lately was to say that every city and town in the US of A should change their street signs so that ALL CAPS are not used and only upper and lower case letters appear. This may or may not be a good idea, but to mandate it to the folks in Axtell or Elk or Waco is ridiculous. To the government, I would say...LEAVE US ALONE! In all caps.

There was some talk recently about Cowboy Poets because Senator Harry Reid was bemoaning the fact that a Cowboy Poet event in Arizona might not get federal government funding. (Oh my God, how will we survive?) Anyway, I wondered if they had a Cowboy Poet contest and there was a National Champion declared...would he be known as the National Poet Lariet?

I am sometimes known as a purveyor of lawyer jokes. But when my youngest daughter, Lauren, graduated from law school...I was encouraged to knock it off. So, I no longer tell lawyer jokes. Just the occasional Attorney Anecdote.

Is America a great country or what? Where else could you find a lawyer to sue McDonalds and Wendy's and Burger King because you ate too many hamburgers and french fries and became vertically challenged? (Spell-check always wants me to capitalize "french", but since we are talking about potatoes, I don't want to. When the French become our friends, I'll think about it.)

STOP ME BEFORE I SUPERSIZE AGAIN! It was inevitable. There are only a limited number of folks who weren't really hurt by asbestos or who weren't really hurt by silicone implants who are willing to sue the people who didn't really hurt them. For instance, finding males who have had breast implants is difficult even for Texas trial lawyers. The number of folks who weigh more than medical charts indicate they should, however, is staggering. It's approximately 328,762 times the number of lawyers who graduated from law school last year. That's way too many. Lawyers and chart-busters.

It may be OK to occasionally super-size or mega-size but don't hypothesize – it could make you "the size of a hippo."

You may have seen news of a recent lawsuit filed in Canada. A father sued an amateur hockey association for $300,000 because his son didn't win the Most Valuable Player award. He said that his son suffered psychological damage and potential career damage. I think that this may set a most valuable precedent.

I'm making plans to sue my high school graduating class. There must be at least one of those slackers with deep pockets. They didn't elect me "Most Handsome" thereby hurting my self-esteem and actually making me "Less Handsome". They didn't elect me "Most Popular" which certainly effectuated a lifetime of LPS (Low Popularity Syndrome). Nor did they elect me "Most Likely to Succeed." While this exhibited an excellent power of prophecy, it obviously destroyed my future financial opportunities. I figure with a couple of million dollars of jury award, I will be much more popular, viewed as more handsome and will have beaten that financial bugaboo.

The elections are upon us. Just wondering...when did we give the people of Absentia the right to vote? And speaking of voting, it's odd to think that there was a time in this country when women couldn't vote. I mean, come on...how hard was it to vote, for crying out loud?

There's a criminal lawyer in the office next door to mine. He sometimes explains some of the finer points of criminal law to me. Just a thought. If you ever decide to murder someone, don't do yoga beforehand. That pre-meditation thing seems to make a big difference in court.

The Texas legislature, in the recent not-so-special-session, has passed a new tax on cigarettes. They did it for the money, but hopefully it will also discourage younger folks from starting to smoke. People say that cigarette smoke causes cancer, but that's not really true. It's not the smoke, it's breathing-in the smoke that causes cancer. So, if you just stop breathing, the odds are great that you won't ever get cancer.

Speaking of the legislature...in the capitol building in Austin, the bathrooms have hot air hand-drying machines. Someone put a sticky-note on a machine that said; "Push here for brief message from your state representative."

You probably heard about the lawsuit to remove the Ten Commandments monument from the state capitol grounds. It wasn't really about the separation of church and state, but it turns out that posting "Thou Shalt Not Steal" near a building full of lawyers and politicians was creating a hostile work environment.

I heard that there's an association called Attorneys For Asbestos Injury. Hey, at least they're honest about it.

Speaking of lawyers, a lawyer friend of mine (OK, a lawyer acquaintance of mine) said he would never again accept a retainer for his services from a client who was an orthodontist.

In the recent election, hats off to Senator Kay Bailey Hutchison. As far as I know, she didn't run a single TV commercial or radio commercial or newspaper ad or do any billboards or have any recorded phone calls. I guess she ran on her reputation and record. She got 67% of the vote. Did I ever mention that when I was a student at The University, Kay Bailey was a cheerleader? She was "hot" before that term had been used to describe attractive females. Of course, Rick Perry was also a cheerleader at A&M. (OK, OK a YELL leader!) He might have been "warm." I don't know, you'd have to ask an Aggie.

In other election news...a Libertarian candidate for Texas Senate, Phil Smart, said that serving a little time in jail right before the election had helped him because of the free publicity. Well...his name may be Smart, but...you know. If he ever gets in trouble again, it would be worth going to his trial just to see what a jury of his peers looked like.

WHO WOULD HAVE MORE EXCITING PARTIES? LIBERTARIANS OR LIBRARIANS?

You probably heard about the bird crisis in Austin. The day before the invasion of the legislature, downtown Austin, close to the Capitol, was invaded by dead birds, mostly Grackles. It's not really known if they committed suicide in a horrid anticipation of the legislative session. They may have. We just don't know. As is most everything in Austin, however, this was a crisis. A very serious crisis. They shut down several blocks of downtown to determine what had killed the birds. As usual, the folks in Austin had their priorities exactly backwards. They were trying to find out what killed the Grackles so that they could stop it. They should have been trying to find out what killed the Grackles so they could encourage it. We'll pay good money for whatever it is in Waco.

What did we do before the popularity of the refrigerator magnet? Where in the world did we put all of that stuff? Some day someone will be killed when their refrigerator just falls over on top of them because it was overloaded with magnetized stuff. This will, of course, create a new career field for lawyers. Can't you just see the TV commercials? "Have you or your loved ones been killed or injured by a falling magnet-stuffed refrigerator? If so call Honest Abe Johnson at 1-800-SUE-A-FRIGE."

You're aware of the recent lawsuits against fast food and fat food and fast fat food. (Food may be the only thing that's both fat and fast.) This kind of lawsuit is the way the ban on smoking in restaurants started. The logical extension of this process is that someday soon when we go to a restaurant, they will ask "Eating or Non-Eating." I'm not sure what will happen in the Non-Eating section. How will the waitperson know when you're through?

You may have heard about a McDonald's employee in Georgia getting arrested for putting too much salt on a hamburger. Now this is crime fighting at its best. The employee said she spilled salt on the meat accidentally and tried to scrape it off. But, unfortunately for her, she served the salt-laden hamburger to a policeman. The policeman said it made him sick and he came back later and arrested the cook on a misdemeanor charge of "reckless conduct." Thank God she didn't serve it to a lawyer. Then things would have really gotten salty.

A policeman arrived at the scene of an accident where a man had run into a tree. The went to the car and asked the man, "Are you seriously injured?" The man said, "How would I know, I'm not a lawyer."

Speaking of police, a local policeman was called to a day care center where a child was resisting a rest.

Have there ever been as many presidential debates as there have been this year? No, there haven't. I haven't watched too many of them, but have seen a lot of replays and I think that the debates could take a page from college and pro football. If one candidate thinks another candidate said something really wrong or stupid, he could throw out a red flag and challenge the statement. The re-play officials would run the tape back, check out what he (or she) said and rule if it was a bald-faced lie or just something stupid. If caught in either, there would be a yellow penalty flag thrown and the candidate would have to back up ten yards and start over.

In the old days, allegedly, a lot of political decisions were made in "smoke-filled rooms." I don't know why the rooms were identified as "smoke-filled," because back in the 40's and 50's and 60's most all rooms were "smoke-filled" because most everyone was smoking. Today, of course, nobody is smoking in a room, unless it's their house and their spouse is gone. Today the only smoke-filled rooms are Mexican restaurants that serve sizzling fajitas...and even that is irritating.

I heard a politician say that he wasn't very good a "small-talk." I noticed that he wasn't very good at "large-talk" either.

It is so strange listening to members of congress and the crazy things that they say. Sometimes I think that if idiots grew on trees, Congress would be an orchard.

The next time I get an email from a Nigerian prince who wants to give me millions of dollars, I'm going to forward it to members of congress. They could use it to reduce the national debt or to fund the Cowboy Poet contest.

If the top doctor and top lawyer in the US government are called the Surgeon General and the Attorney General, how come the person who heads up the military is called the Secretary of Defense? Can he type really fast? Besides, the word "secretary" is not PC. Shouldn't he at least be the Administrative Assistant of Defense?

Speaking of the federal government, the First Lady, and others, are very active in trying to deal with childhood obesity. Good for them. Here's a suggestion. At summer camps the kids should probably sit around the campfire and roast s'lesses.

A friend said that he got some bad news recently that his newborn nephew was born with a defective heart. But he said the good news was that they had never had a lawyer in the family before.

Speaking of lawyers, I'd bet the worst part of being U2's lawyer is having to do everything pro Bono.

Did you ever think that the phrase, "lefty loosey, righty tighty" not only applies to nuts, but also to politics? Of course, there are a lot of nuts in politics.

Sometimes you feel like a nut. Sometimes you remember to take your meds.

Speaking of politics and nuts, I heard about a couple who were so liberal that they tried to adopt a gay baby. If there is ever a book written about gay adoption, it should be called: *"It Takes a Village, People!"*

Our government throws around the "trillion" dollar figure a lot. How much is a trillion? The average life span is about 2.8 billion seconds. To live to a trillion seconds, you would have to be 31 thousand years old. Methuselah was only 969 years old. A trillion seconds is Methuselah times 32. I'm guessing that Methuselah died of old age. Either that or a skateboard accident.

You probably heard about the post office running out of money and the chance that they might just shut down the whole thing for a lack of business. I think we should start a protest or a petition drive to save the post office. I would suggest that we do it by email.

In about nine months, we will be voting for a President and a bunch of other candidates for office. Are you tired already? The Republican's presidential candidates have offered some fun this year. It's possible that Herman Cain dropped out of the race to spend more time with your wife. And speaking of wives...Newt Gingrich may define "traditional marriage" as "One man, one woman and one staffer." Newt also said something about being able to arrest judges. I guess that multiple divorces can make you hate judges.

I think that Rick Perry had three good things going for him. Good hair, good suits....and I can't remember the third thing.

Did you read that it costs our government two and a half cents to manufacture a penny? It also costs 11 cents to make a nickel. This is shocking. The US Mint used to be the only government agency that "made money." Now they lose money while making money. Only in America. Forget the "shocking" comment. What does the government do that is cost effective? If they are only losing 80% of the cost of making a penny, that's probably better than most government programs. The mint should get an efficiency award. Canada had a similar problem, so they quit making pennies. In our government, losing vast amounts of money while making money is not a problem. It's a government thing. We wouldn't understand.

Not only is the penny perhaps going away, but what happened to the "cent" symbol? (You know, the "C" with a line through it.) I can't find that symbol on my computer keyboard. On my old typewriter the "cent" sign was on the same key with the "6." On my computer keyboard the capital 6 will yield a ^. I don't know what a ^ is, but I've never used it. So now if I want to put in my two cents worth, I have to put in my $.02. I want my cent key back. Who do I call? If you think you know, I'll give you a penny for your thought.

I'm sure you heard about the workers at the federal mint in Ft. Worth who went on strike. They wanted to make less money.

I know you've heard about the political dog wars. Governor Romney drove on the highway (30 something years ago) with his dog in a crate on top of the car. The dog wasn't hurt. (With 4 little boys in the car, the dog may have asked to ride on top.) President Obama, in his book Dreams of My Father, said that when he was a boy growing up in Indonesia (30 something years ago), he ate dog meat (and grasshoppers). When asked about it Hillary Rosen said that it was OK for the President to eat dog meat because it was probably a stay-at-home dog and had never worked a day in its life. Just kidding. This may well be the strangest presidential campaign ever. Let's don't discuss the debt or deficit. Let's talk about 30 year old dog stories. I'll bet that Romney has also driven with a grasshopper in his car grill. So we're all even.

According to the polls, and according to common sense, congress is not too popular. They're ranked somewhere between rattle snakes and migraine headaches, so this story just might be true. A driver was stuck in a traffic jam on the highway outside of Washington, DC. Nothing was moving. Suddenly, a man knocked on his window. The driver rolls down the window and asked, "What's going on?" The other man said, "Terrorists have kidnapped the entire US Congress, and they're asking for a $100 million dollar ransom. Otherwise, they say they are going to douse them all in gasoline and set them all on fire." The driver asked, "About how much is everyone giving?" The man replies, "About a gallon."

I read a news report that said that the North Koreans have up to twenty underground airports. Underground airports? It's no wonder the North Koreans are starving. Next they will have aboveground subways, or aboveways. If they get well above ground, they can become highways.) Asians are generally thought to be the smartest race of humans. Don't know what happened to the North Koreans. I guess that stupid leaders can make the whole country stupid. Don't think too much about that possibility.

Following up on the previous paragraph...VP Joe Biden recently gave a speech to a high school graduation in Miami. He told the students to "imagine" a lot of things that would happen in the next 40 years of their lifetimes. Among other things for them to imagine were: "...crops that don't depend on the soil, water or fertilizer or pesticides...." He said it was "just around the corner". I guess the crops will just grow in the air. I'm familiar with an air-horn, but not air-corn. He also said to imagine: "...when in your lifetimes, doctors are able to regenerate entire body organs and limbs that have been damaged or lost". We'll be able to just grow a heart or an arm or a leg? I think he's pulling our leg. He also said to imagine that we would have a roof on our house made entirely of solar panels that would power our heating and cooling and run our appliances and would cost no more than the regular shingles that we use today. I haven't priced shingles lately (or ever), but they must be awfully high. Maybe their price has gone "through the roof."

Did you hear about the President's re-election campaign suggesting that instead of getting wedding, anniversary or birthday gifts that you should encourage your friends and relatives to send money to the Obama Campaign instead? I'm not making this up. Here is exactly what the ad said:

Obama Event Registry

Got a birthday, wedding or anniversary coming up? Let your friends know how important this election is to you – register with Obama 2012, and ask for a donation in lieu of a gift. It's a great way to support the President on your big day. Plus, it's a gift we can all appreciate – and goes a lot further than a gravy bowl. Setting up and sharing your registry page is easy – so get started today.

Now that's just plain weird. You wonder who thought of it. Why would you not want your own wedding gifts or birthday presents? On my wedding day, I had things on my mind other than political donations. And the only thing wrong with a gravy bowl is if it's empty. Gravy (at least cream gravy) should be one of the food groups. A good gravy bowl will last decades longer than politicians. We hope.

Speaking of the President, he recently invoked Executive Privilege to protect some documents that he didn't think congress needed to see. I think there should be executive privilege for husbands. When asked if I wanted to go shopping, I could invoke my husband's executive privilege. Of course, a higher local court would then determine that I had lost that privilege along with several others.

Many years ago, when our kids were young, we had a poster that had a fun list of collective nouns for animals. Terms for groups of animals like a school of fish or a pride of lions. There are some very strange ones, like a flutter of butterflies, a murder of crows, a convocation of eagles, a tower of giraffes, a crash of rhinoceroses and a dazzle of zebras. But perhaps the best name of a group is one option for baboons. It's a "Congress" of baboons. Couldn't have come with a better name myself.

CHAPTER TWO

Tv & Other Alleged Entertainment

It sometimes seems that television ran out of good ideas years ago. I don't think that Celebrity Dancing was as lame as Celebrity Skating, but it's difficult to quantify rubbish. Now there's The Celebrity Cooking Shootout. What next? Celebrity Sewing? Celebrity House Cleaning? Celebrity Waiting in the Doctor's Office? And who are these people and when were they celebrities?

There are many TV shows that I don't want to watch and for some of them, I don't even want to watch their promos. "Survivor" promos, for instance, irritate me. A bunch of really nasty people in really dirty places doing really strange things. The contestants apparently hope to get filthy, stinking rich. Well, they've got 2 out of 3 down already.

For some unexplainable reason a lot of people are addicted to television reality shows. I think a good idea for a new reality show might be to show a bunch of people sitting around watching reality shows.

Are reality shows getting worse or are there just more of them? It has been said for years that TV programming is aimed at a 12-year-old level. This year I think it might be time to ask…a 12-year-old what?

. Wouldn't you like to hear a TV weatherperson say, "Tomorrow it will be partly cloudy and hot with a 20% chance of rain and a 50% chance that I'm wrong".

I noticed a TV commercial for a sleeping pill that listed several potential negative side effects. One was "drowsiness." Who'd have thought it?

I haven't seen too many of the new TV shows for this year, but I have read about them. They mostly sound like something you couldn't watch with your kids or parents or preacher. I would recommend to the TV show producers to try thinking inside the box and to leave the envelope alone. Don't push it.

Speaking of TV, I heard a TV investment guy recommend cattle futures. I'm not going to do it. Their futures don't seem so promising to me.

At all of the college football games, cameras pan the sidelines and find students on the bottom rows who have their faces and bodies painted and are wearing freakish clothes or not much clothes at all. When the camera approaches, the students almost fall out of the stands to attack the camera lens with screams and hand signs and wild gesticulations making them appear to be completely mentally defective. They do this even when their team is losing by a score of 50 to nothing. What are their parents thinking? I'm paying $30,000 to send my kid to college and this is what I get? Maybe the networks could just show us the game? And please spare me from the announcers who constantly say… "If he hadn't of tripped and fallen on his face at the 50 yard line, he would have gone ALL THE WAY." Or maybe one of the 11 other athletes on the field (12 at A&M) would have tackled him?

I saw a commercial for a teeth-whitening product in which a spokesperson claimed to be a cashier at a coffee shop. She said she often had customers with coffee stained teeth and she always recommended product X to them to solve their problem. There's a great concept. Insult your customers by telling them that their teeth are ugly. Waitresses in restaurants could tell customers that they can't have the chicken fried steak and they really should have a salad with no dressing and a dry baked potato cause they are way too fat. Convenience store clerks could tell customers that they can't have that 12 pack of beer because they look like they would probably do something stupid. We could call it "Customer Disservice."

I was watching another arrest of a criminal on TV and, as always, the policeman pushed down on the head of the criminal getting into the back seat of the police car. Why do they do that? Do felons suddenly forget how to bend over once they're arrested? Do they usually bump their heads? Is this what drove them to crime?

I think that CSI was the most watched TV show in the country this last year. It's pretty good. I like the Vegas version more than the Miami version. These are very smart people using the very latest scientific knowledge and gadgets to solve crimes. The investigators are brilliant with one exception. They don't know how to turn on lights. They go into a room or a building and hold their flashlights beside their heads and use them until the batteries are gone. Hey guys, just turn the lights on.

HOW MANY CSI'S DOES IT TAKE TO CHANGE A LIGHT BULB? NO ONE KNOWS, THEY'VE NEVER USED ONE.

Do you ever watch CSI Miami? It's my least favorite of the three CSI shows. If people who watch this show ever go to Miami they will be disappointed that Miami isn't all bright blue, yellow, orange and green. In the TV show, all of the colors are enhanced and distorted to a highly unreal degree. Nothing is gray or brown or tan or white, it's all unnatural, weird colors. Why do they do that? It's like they are playing with some new computer color program that they bought.

There is nothing in my training or background that would allow me to judge the relative strength of actors, but I think that the lead actor on CSI Miami, David Caruso, is the worst actor on TV. Nothing he does is natural, including walking, talking or standing.

Speaking of bad acting, a friend said that he saw a movie that was so bad; he actually got up and walked out on it. But, since he had rented the movie, he had to just hang out in his back yard till it was over.

Speaking of television, and bad acting, I am the moderator of a TV show called "Challenge" which is an academic quiz show for area high school students. (I'm not a real quiz show host, but I play one on TV.) Anyway, the questions are very hard. I not only can't answer them, I have trouble just reading them. I have to practice pronouncing many words with which I am unfamiliar. But, I do learn things that I never knew. For instance, I learned that photons have mass. Heck, I didn't even know they were catholic.

I read that the first choice to replace Rosie O'Donnell on The View (a show that I have never seen) is Roseanne Barr. Have you ever seen those two together? I think that they're the same person. I hope so. Two of them is too many.

I watched a little of the Miss Universe pageant, and I've got a feeling that it's rigged. Every single year the winner is from Earth.

Another somewhat interesting summer TV show is "America's Got Talent". David Hasselhoff is one of the judges. Should David Hasselhoff really be judging other people's talents? Is that kind of like getting hair styling advice from Donald Trump?"
Speaking of Donald Trump, I saw a bald eagle at the zoo. He had all of his feathers combed over to one side. (Yes, yes, I know... he who is without sin...)

I was watching a TV ad for a hot new action-packed movie. It said it would be opening on October 15th and "Only in Theaters". I'm glad they added that information, because I was thinking of trying to catch the movie at my local auto parts store. Or accountant's office. Or bus stop.

There's a TV commercial for some home security system in which a husband and wife are lying in bed and all of a sudden there is an unusual noise, which sounds exactly like a burglar breaking into the house. The wife sits up and says, "Did you hear that?" The husband says, "It's our first night in our new house, do you think I should check?" If I had written that commercial, I would then have the wife say, "No, stupid. Since it's our first night in our new house, I don't think you should check. Since it's our first night in our new house I think that we should let the burglar rob, plunder and pillage us, you blithering idiot!" Thank goodness they had a security system, cause they could still be discussing how long they had lived in the house and what to do about it while their big screen was being loading into a van.

Another TV ad that drives me crazy. There is an ad for one of those "you know what" products that shows two adults, apparently in their birthday suits, reclining in two antique bathtubs which are apparently in their back yard, enjoying a beautiful view. Who would put two old bathtubs in their back yard? Have they heard about hot tubs? Who fills the tubs with water? How cold is the water? How dirty is the water? What about mosquitoes? Do the dogs drink out of the tubs? What are the neighbors in the two- story house next-door thinking? How dumb is this couple? How dumb do they think we are? I think that the cold, dirty, mosquito attracting, dog serving water would overcome whatever the intension of the "you know what" pill is.

Have you noticed that televised football games (and almost all of them are these days) take about 6 hours to play? This is because of the inordinate number of TV commercials. It is particularly irritating to me when someone scores and then they break for 4 minutes of commercials. Then they come back, have the kickoff, and then go to another 4 minutes of commercials. They don't interrupt baseball games for commercials except between innings. They don't interrupt basketball games except during timeouts. But at football games, the TV people control the game, not the other way around. Who do you call? I want to throw a fit and a penalty flag.

All of the timeouts for commercials give you too much time to think of other things, like the fact that Tony Romo spelled backwards is Ynot Omor. Well, why not Omor? I don't know. It was bad luck for the Cowboys that Tony broke his little finger. Some people are just unlucky. Like the guy who wrote a catchy song that never made it. It was called "Hi Dolly".

Christmas has come and gone and we can now avoid the TV commercials for weird products that we don't need and get back to commercials for medicines that we don't need.

The best way to tell that Christmas is approaching is when you begin to see TV commercials for men's electric razors. You would think that men only use electric razors during the Christmas holidays. Maybe it's true.

Did you see the commercial for "Snuggies"? A "Snuggie" is a blanket that someone, for no apparent reason, sewed together to make two arm holes (one for each arm). You then wear the blanket, not only when lying down watching TV in your den, but also on bleachers while watching an outdoor soccer game with the whole fam damily. The man in the commercial looks like some sort of deranged monk. The family at the soccer game looks like members of some weird cult who have been listening to voices that no one else hears that said, "Dress like fools and go to a soccer game!" One scene shows a Mom and her daughter who is about 5 years old lying down together on the couch wearing the lovely Snuggies and the ad says of the "extra large" Snuggies that "one size fits all". No it doesn't. The six year old, who is about 3 and 1/2 feet tall, couldn't possibly walk with her Snuggie on and to wear a queen sized blanket, you need to be at least queen sized.

Sometimes I think that these products aren't real. Maybe someone in the government puts the ads on TV and then keeps track of anyone who tries to order them and puts those people on some sort of moron watch list. It's part of the Homeland Security effort to monitor nincompoops. If they would buy a Snuggie, goodness knows what else they might do.

I have a friend who almost never watches live TV. He records everything to watch later so he can fast-forward through the commercials. I don't know how widespread this is, but it's not good news for advertisers. There are several TV commercials that I really enjoy. Some show the incredible things that can be done with technology. For instance, have you seen the Travelers ad that shows all of the wild animals playing with each other on the riverbank? I can't imagine how they produced that. Then there's the new spot for Accenture (whoever that is) that shows a surfing elephant. And my favorite is the E-Trade singing babies. We've all known that you can't believe what you hear, but these commercials all prove that you can't believe what you see either. It's almost like the national network news. I also love the Geico (put the I before the E except for insurance companies) ads with the little piggy that goes "Wee Wee Wee" all the way home and the antique road show look-a-like where the woman brings in a ceramic "bird in a hand." She's thrilled when the appraiser tells her that it's worth at least "two in the bush."

I watched one of those irritating promos for some wrestling pay-for-view event. The announcer said about one of the contestants, "No one has ever been able to body-slam this giant of a man!" That sounded pretty impressive until it occurred to me that I've never been body-slammed either and I'm not even a wrestler!

Speaking of watching TV, I think that I'm probably about average. I watch a lot. I like to have one on even if I'm not paying much attention. (You never know when something important might happen like a flash flood watch while the sun is still shining or someone taking a hostage in New

Jersey or police car chase in Los Angeles.) But based on the Emmy's, I might as well not have a TV. Winning shows included Breaking Bad, Nurse Jackie, Top Chef, Temple Grandin and You Don't Know Jack. Not only had I not seen any of these shows, I had never heard of them. I had heard of other winners (Glee, Big Bang Theory, Modern Family, Dexter, The Daily Show) but had never watched them. Eight shows on HBO won Emmy's and I don't have HBO. The only two shows that I watch regularly that won for anything were The Good Wife and The Closer. Is there something wrong with me, or the folks who choose the winners? It seems that the less viewers a show has, the more likely it is to win an Emmy. But then, maybe I don't know Jack.

I was listening to a TV ad about hearing aides and their importance to a good life. I wondered if anyone has thought about inventing a "talking aide". A little battery operated thing you put in your mouth. A lot of people hear better than they talk. Maybe a talking aide could take away my Texas twang, correct grammatical errors, and control the volume. They say that talk is cheap. It's because it exceeds the demand.

Have you noticed lately that most of TV's leading men don't shave? The guys on Hawaii 5-0 and Dr. House, for instance, always have about a week's growth of beard. Most of the male models that you see in magazines have beard stubble. How did this get to be cool? I would say either grow a beard or don't. A scratchy face is an unhappy face. At first I didn't like my beard, but then it grew on me.

Researchers in Australia say that for every hour you watch TV after age 25, you lose 22 minutes of your life. If that were true, I'd be but a pleasant memory to the funeral home director. Maybe it just works in Australia. If you watch too much TV Down Under you go down under a lot sooner. This study is so stupid that I'm shocked that the US Government didn't pay for it.

When it rains (some of you will remember rain) while the sun is shining (you all will know about the shining sun), we used to say that the devil was whipping his wife. Where did that come from? First of all the devil isn't in close proximity to the rain clouds. He is somewhat lower down (as though he watched too much TV in Australia). And then too, where is it written that the devil is married? Who would marry a red man with horns and a pointy tail? Maybe Madonna or Lady Gaga?

There's a fairly new ad on TV for a product called Sensa. You just shake it on your food, like salt, and then eat the food and you lose weight.

I don't know what it is, but it must be some magic potion. Maybe it shrinks the food. Maybe it tastes so bad you won't eat the food. Think how much weight you could lose if you just shook the Sensa into your mouth and didn't eat anything. If it sounds too good to be true....

Another TV commercial that I've seen a hundred times is a guy who comes on the screen and says, "My name is Doug and I have mesothelioma." I feel sorry for Doug, but I think he should spend less time with his lawyer and more with a doctor.

I saw a TV commercial for a refrigerator with a built-in TV set on the front. For those folks who have been standing around watching their refrigerators for entertainment, this will be a great addition.

CHAPTER THREE

Really Random Thoughts

These thoughts are too random to categorize, so they are just random, random thoughts.

There was a big thunderstorm alarm about a month ago. The TV weather folks tend to scare you to death in the anticipation of imminent destruction. I guess it's better to be safe than sorry. Anyway, that night, there was a serious threat of serious storms. I was home alone and things were pretty quiet when all of a sudden, there was a loud noise that sounded like a freight train passing through my neighborhood. My first thought was "Oh, no...a tornado". Then I realized that it was a freight train...the same one that goes down the track about a block and a half from my house every night about this time". It's amazing how much those freight trains sound just like freight trains.

They say if you don't like the weather in Texas, just wait a minute. The same is true of medical studies. If you don't like one, just wait awhile, it will change.

A recent study said that an apple a day will keep the Doctor away. But, that it is specifically the skin of a Red Delicious apple that will do you the most good. I much prefer green Granny Smith green apples to Red Delicious apples, so I'm going to just wait on the next study.

I wonder why I frequently go back to the refrigerator thinking that something new will show up?

The Triple Crown of horse racing is over for the year with no one single winner. I really enjoy watching horse races but other races, I'm not so sure about. I've never been to a car race, but they are, I think, the nation's largest spectator sport. I am pretty sure I don't want to go to a Greyhound race. How exciting could it be to watch a bunch of big buses rumble around a track? And then there's drag racing. Watching men in high heels and dresses race each other? I don't think so.

There is apparently a franchise of some sort for "Dummy" books. "Computers for Dummies", "Cooking for Dummies", "Taxes for Dummies." The books are yellow and black and have a very similar look, so it must be some sort of franchise deal. I think I have a couple of ideas that might really sell. How about "Professional Wrestling for Dummies." Surely somebody could get rich with a "Jerry Springer for Dummies." Seems like a natural to me.

I enjoy reading the obituaries in the local newspaper. It used to be that funeral homes filled out an information form and sent it to the newspaper where the obituary-writer (not the most sought-after newspaper job) would write the information into a standard, fill-in-the-blanks-type obituary. But since the newspaper started charging (so much per word) for obituaries, people now write their own and they are much more interesting. You can find several euphemisms for "dying". The most common (based on my survey of at least two days of obituaries) term is " so-and-so 'died' on June 12th". Second most popular is "so-and-so 'passed away'. Other options are "met his Maker", "went to be with her Lord", "passed into Life Eternal ", "entered into eternal rest". I have yet to see "Shuffled off his mortal coil", or "kicked the bucket" or "assumed room temperature" or "began his dirt nap", but one never knows. We get much more interesting information about the deceased than we used to. More personal, more fun things. I also like the trend of putting a picture of the person when he or she was about 30 years old and in his or her prime. Seeing the picture of a young, smiling WWII soldier in uniform warms my heart. Or a picture of a smiling young woman with her hair in a bun, 1940's style, brings back memories of what must have been a happier time.

A few years ago a local obituary reported "So-and-so died in his home on June 12th." That statement was true, as far as it went. In that particular case, "So-and-so" was a criminal who had died at the hands of the local gendarmes. A more correct obituary would have said, "So-and-so died in his home on June 12th under a hail of bullets from a swat-team." I guess that wasn't an option on the obit form.

I recently noticed an article written by a local "retired gerontologist." I wondered why a gerontologist would retire. Wouldn't they just get better as they got older? Wouldn't a 95-year-old gerontologist be better than a 65-year-old gerontologist? Just wondered.

I also recently read an article in a newspaper about a couple celebrating their 50th wedding anniversary. It said that the husband had retired from XYZ Company and that his wife was a "retired homemaker." My guess is that approximately 112 million women, in the United States alone, want to know where you go to file those homemaker retirement papers.

Speaking of women, and we were, since there's so much money to be made by catering to soon-to-be and new mothers, I wonder why someone hasn't started a fitness center called the OB-GYM? They could take their newborns with them and do sit-ups and spit-ups at the same time.

Sometimes while driving around Waco, I daydream about what I would do if I won the lottery. As a member of the "nouveau riche" (a difficult-to-pronounce way of saying "newly rich" in French) I would have lots of new options. One would be to never again say anything in French. France doesn't want to be our friend and I think we should return the favor. Everything French other than fries should be discouraged. The word "lottery" itself came to us from the French word "loterie," which is an example of the fact that the French can't even spell well. One of my favorite political columnists, Jonah Goldberg, calls the French "cheese-eating-surrender-monkeys." I don't understand exactly what that means, but I concur wholeheartedly.

The lottery has been called "a tax on people who are bad at math." While it is true that your odds of winning the Texas lottery are about one in 21 million, it is also true that about once every couple of weeks somebody does win. It could be me.

Anyway, if I won the lottery, there are several things I would do. (1) I would just throw away a toothpaste tube when it is so empty that it's a pain to continue squeezing it. (2) I would just throw away soap slivers when they got so small that I drop them in the shower. (3) I would pay somebody to go through newly arrived magazines to tear out all of the annoying subscription cards. (4) I would buy a new Teflon skillet when most of the Teflon is gone on the old one. (5) I would consider putting aluminum siding on my house.

Speaking of those from other countries (as in France), one very frequent question in the last few months concerning Bin Laden and his cohorts is "Why do they hate us so?" The obvious answer is "Who cares?" but that answer doesn't satisfy everyone. After watching the videotape of Bin Laden and his friends sitting around the cave or tent or palace, a good reason for their hatred seemed to appear. They hate us because we have chairs and they don't. If I sit on the floor for more than two minutes and try to get up, I get a little cranky myself. Maybe if we airlifted some furniture to these folks, they would mellow out.

I also heard the sad news reported that some Afghan refugees were in such bad shape that they were resorting to eating grass. This astounded me. Not that they would eat grass, but that they could find some grass to eat. I haven't seen any in the TV news video. Maybe we could send "Chia-Pet Chairs" and kill two birds with one stone.

There are many things that have been called "the greatest thing since sliced bread". There are at least a couple of generations of folks who don't understand the significance of this phrase. We've never really had to slice bread. Mrs. Baird did it and does it for us, and she is much better at it than we were or are. Yeah, some French bread loafs (didn't I discourage all things French earlier?) are un-sliced, but they are small and fairly easy. Anyway, the point is that "sliced bread" as an example of a wonderful new invention is anachronistic. So the question is...what newer invention should replace "sliced bread" as a milestone of modern convenience?

How about microwave popcorn? How about peel and stick postage stamps? How about talk radio? How about "luxury boxes" at hot September or cold December football games? (I've never sat in one, but I am readily available to personally analyze this innovation as a service for devoted Wacoan readers.) How about Tivo that allows you to pause and/or rewind live TV when the phone rings? How about padded church pews? How about zip lock bags?

I guess that we would appreciate the "sliced bread" deal more if we really had to slice bread ourselves. Fortunately, we don't have to because inventors gradually developed better and better means of slicing bread. First it was one loaf at a time, then an entrepreneur developed the two-loaf knife and then the three-loaf knife and finally he came up with a knife that would slice four loafs of bread at one time. It was the world's first Four-Loaf-Cleaver. I report, you deride.

At our house we recently had a commode that would continue to run until you jiggled the handle. It was annoying, but not quite annoying enough to call a plumber. I took the top off and looked at the inter-workings. Looking was the best I could do, but didn't seem to help. Strangely, after a week or so, the problem stopped. It just quit doing it. It was a clear case of "Self-Plumerization". This word came to mind because I've heard John Morris, the Voice of the Bears, refer to the situation when a running back falls down without being touched as "Self-Tackleization". (John says the phrase originated in the fertile mind of Frank Fallon.) By the way, if John is the "Voice" of the Bears, who are the "Eyes" of the Bears and the "Ears" of the Bears?

One of my favorite philosophic rules is "Occams' Razor". This philosophy was sprouted by William of Occam. I'm not sure where Occam is, but I think you go to Lufkin and turn left. (Just ask for William.) Occam's Razor basically says that when looking at two competing theories, the simplest one is usually the more correct. Insurance companies have quit writing homeowners insurance in Texas because of Black Mold and Texas Trial Lawyers. I have a simple one-word solution to this crisis. Clorox. William would agree.

I THOUGHT THAT HAVING A 5-K RACE TO CALL AWARENESS TO MALE PATTERN BALDNESS WAS A GREAT IDEA, BUT I WAS TOLD THE IDEA WAS BALDERDASH.

Some friends of mine recently went to a football game in a small town not too far from Waco. (I'll keep it a secret so that the school won't be inundated by ACLU types.) Before the game the Superintendent spoke on the public address system. He said, "Ladies and Gentlemen, as you know, the Supreme Court has ruled that we can't pray before football games. I believe in following the law. However, if I were to pray...I would pray for... (and he then gave a very nice prayer)." Don't try to make a living out-slickin' country folks.

I read awhile back of an unusual Central Texas wedding. It was on a golf course. (I wonder if anybody tried to "play through?") The wedding also had an unusual participant, as the couple's dog served as the "Flower Dog". That dog must be much better trained than mine. My dog would have barked incessantly, eaten the flowers, chased a squirrel, jumped on the preacher, destroyed the wedding cake and treated the flag stick like a fire hydrant. And all of that before the reception.

The Governor of Alabama got in trouble recently for saying that "If God had wanted boys to wear earrings, he would have made them girls." I'm not too sure about his theology, but he does seem to have an eye for fashion. I too have trouble understanding the fashion choices of young men. I taught a class at Baylor for a couple of semesters and never saw the top of the heads of any of my male students. They never removed their baseball caps. Ever. When I was young (and also when I was in the Army) you didn't wear a hat inside. I wonder when the rule changed?

Someone asked the question, "Why do we have 50 candidates for Miss America and only 2 for President?" It's a good question, especially since the Miss America contest is limited to people of a certain age, gender and shape. The Presidency is open to almost anybody, as Ralph Nader and Pat Buchanan proved. Maybe it's because we expect more from Miss America. She has to answer current event questions and sing or dance or play the piano or twirl a baton.

As this is written, the Waco Silly Council is again confronted with a major policy decision. Should the name of Indian Spring Park, the home of the wonderful summer concerts, be changed? Some folks want Martin Luther King Park, now on the other side of the river and cleverly placed on MLK Boulevard, to cross the Suspension Bridge and occupy both sides of the river. In that bridging of the two sides of the river there would be some symbology, it is said. On the other hand a dozen or so local American Indians protested the suggested name change saying that Indian Spring Park is a park cleverly named after an Indian spring where the Waco Indians created an early settlement and that the name has cultural significance to the local American Indians.

This is confusing. Indians in places like Cleveland protest the use of the word "Indians" as disrespectful. Waco Indians are apparently less PC and more CT (clear thinking). With the wisdom of King Solomon, the Council could combine the names. The park could be called the Martin Indian Luther Spring King Park. The public would probably abbreviate it to Spring King Park and in May there could be a festival to name Waco's

Spring King. The male contestants would have to answer current event questions and sing or dance or play the piano or twirl a baton.

I read of a new problem lately. Some people have too much house. You know, the kids move out and the couple just doesn't need that much room, that much upkeep or that much expense. So from now on you should not only be concerned for the homeless, but also for the homemore. Maybe the homemores could rent rooms to the homeless.

Childproof medicine bottles are a good idea. Adult proof candy wrappers are not. Vicki and I were at a movie recently and I bought some Skittles. I could not open the package. I figured that if I pulled any harder, the bag would pop open scattering my Skittles throughout the theater. Some of the folks probably wouldn't have appreciated a skittle shower. I gave up. Vicki used her fingernails to finally open the package, but by then I was too tired to eat.

A little girl was trying to open a medicine bottle and failing. She told her Mother that it was too hard to open. The understanding mother explained the concept of "childproof" bottles, and how they were designed so that children couldn't open them. The little girl asked, "How does it know it's me?"

Scientists at A&M are doing better than most at cloning. After about sixty-something tries, they produced a kitten. Wonder why they chose a cat? Is there a cat shortage in College Station? Don't cats seem to do a really good job of propagating their own species? Next thing you know, they'll be cloning grackles. Why don't they clone something useful like snail darters or golden-cheeked warblers? If there were a bunch more of them, maybe people could use their land for whatever they wanted to.

SCIENTIST AT A&M ALSO DISCOVERED RECENTLY THAT DOGS CAN ACTUALLY LIVE UNDER WATER. BUT NOT FOR VERY LONG.

While driving to lunch, I heard a radio commercial advertising "Sedation Dentistry". The pitch was that the dentist would just give you a "small pill" and you would be "almost" asleep" and they could do 12 root canals and you would wake up with sweet dreams and no pain. At least until you got home. If it works, this is really a great idea. I don't hate dentists, but I do hate seeing them in their place of business. The sight of a huge hypodermic needle, that the dentist requires help to lift, just about renders me unconscious (quicker than the small pill) and I can gag just by thinking about someone in a blue smock looking in my mouth.

So I was thinking. If Sedation Dentistry really works, why not try it in other fields. How about Sedation Lawery? You could go to a lawyer, take a small pill, and have sweet dreams while he or she explains why your situation is closer to a solution but will take a little longer than expected and be a little more expensive than expected because the lawyer on the other side has a court appearance in Acapulco (or at least he will be appearing before the bar there after he appears before the beach there) and that this particular visit to your lawyer won't quite solve your problem, but will make his or her car payment a breeze.

How about Sedation IRSery? You take a small pill before going to see the IRS person and sleep through his discussion about why each of your deductions was denied and that federal prisons aren't really that tough anyway.

How about Sedation Tech Supportery? You could call your computer company tech support office, take a "small pill" and wake up three hours later just in time to hear the recorded person tell you that "Your call is very important to us, so please stay on the line. A customer service representative will be with you as soon as a sober one returns from the company picnic."

How about Sedation Seminarary. When your company sends you to a 21 hour, three day seminar at the Odessa Holiday Inn to improve your Total Quality Management Developmental Resource Sensitivity Response to Diversity Mediation Acculturation (or the popular TQMDRSRtDMA Seminar), you could take a "not-so-small-pill" and sleep for three days. You would take the 27 workbooks home in case someone in authority asks you about the seminar, which is highly unlikely.

How about the Sedation Let Me Tell You About My Surgery? You could begin your sweet dreams just prior to the colon part.

Other options might include the Sedation Piano Recitalry, Sedation Mary Kay/Tupperware/Avon Presentationary, Sedation Rush Hour Trafficry and the always-popular Sedation Mother-In-Law Visitry.

Do you ever think that everybody else is out of step but you? I feel that way about digital watches. For the life of me, I just can't understand why everybody in the world doesn't have a digital watch. Why haven't they quit making the kind with the big hand and the little hand and the third hand, which is called the "second" hand? With a digital watch, you don't have to "tell time". It tells you what time it is. It's 3:17. And it tells you the day and the month and it has an alarm and it has a stopwatch and it's so easy. Since you can't wind it up, it can't wind down.

Some awards, you really don't want to win. Elvis was recently named the year's most financially successful dead entertainer. Apparently Elvis is the only person whose death we celebrate rather than his birth. Why is that? His death was very un-special.

Elvis produced some great music, but if someone put a gun to my head and demanded to know my favorite Elvis movie, I guess my silence would be deadly. Was one Elvis movie better than another one? Was one worse than another?

An article in the Scientific American says that theoretical physicists (which are one of my very favorite kinds of physicists) are now seriously discussing whether people can be transported to the past or future. It all started with Einstein's Theory of Relativity, which if I had more time I would explain in depth, but basically Big Al said that the measured interval between two events depends on how fast the observer is moving. The "Twin Paradox" is used as an example. Suppose that Bill and Jill are twins. Jill boards a rocket ship and travels at high speed to a nearby star, and immediately turns around and flies back to Earth (assume the stores were closed), while Bill stays at home watering the yard and feeding the dog. For Jill, the duration of the journey might be, say, one year, but when she returns and steps out of the spaceship, she finds that 10 years have elapsed on Earth (The dog would be 70 years older, but that's a different theory.). Her brother is now nine years older than she is. Jill is ecstatic with being 9 years younger than Bill, cancels her next Botox appointment, and books another space flight.

It's a little late for me to weigh in on the Kevin Steele (former Baylor football coach) situation. It's over and done. There are still, however, some lingering questions. Like, why? I have a theory about why Kevin Steele was let go. It wasn't that he didn't have an MVP. It was that he did have MPB.

Kevin lost his job because he lost his hair. MPB (Male Pattern Baldness) can ruin the brightest of careers. What do the best coaches have in common? Bear Bryant, Darrell Royal, Grant Teaff, Mack Brown, Bob Stoops, and the Bowden family all have or had lots of hair.

R.C. Slocum is on the bubble. His hairline and his coaching options are receding. He may have just enough hair for one more year. (His hair did seem to grow a bit when he beat Oklahoma.)

Tom Landry is an excellent example of the MPB/Coach Career Theory. The "Only Head Coach" the Cowboys had for the first 29 years had a severe problem. The head coach had a coach head problem. He hid it successfully for a long time with that famous hat. But then came Jerry Jones. As they say, "It takes one to know one". Jerry, bald himself, saw through Tom's hat and fired him. Jerry bought a wig and a coach with very important hair and won two Super bowls. Then came Barry Switzer with hair as thin as his moral reputation and after one holdover year (it takes awhile for that much JJ hairspray to dissipate) the Cowboys have been in a slide ever since. Hair today, gone tomorrow.

Last month we discussed hair length and coaching career length. Someone asked if this phenomenon applied in other careers. Yes. Politics. Think of the presidential elections in the last 50 years. Eisenhower and Stevenson were both bald, but Ike hid his head with a helmet in WW II, which gave him the edge. Twice. Kennedy had better hair than Nixon. Nixon had better hair than Humphrey and McGovern. Carter had much better hair than Ford. Reagan had more important hair than Carter and Mondale. Clinton had better hair than Bush and Dole. W had better hair than Gore, but just barely. There were two exceptions. Goldwater had better hair than Johnson but was considered hair-brained. Dukakis had better hair than Bush 41 but Dukakis was only about 5 feet tall and you couldn't see his hair in a crowd of people. Obama had better hair than McCain, but Romney had more hair than Obama...but no theory is perfect..

Last month we talked about hair and politics. An email suggested that I was wrong and in fact, Al Gore had better hair than the President and that's why Al won the popular vote. Since I disagree, I think we'll have to take this to the Supreme Court (actually maybe a Hairpellate Court would work. Hairpellate courts are the ones where they open the proceedings by saying, "Hair Ye, Hair Ye, Order in the Court".

Here's a way to win a bet from a friend. (Lawyers can win a bet from an acquaintance.) Casually mention that it's odd that the numbers on a phone and a calculator are not arranged the same way. They will bet you that you're wrong. You'll be right. On a calculator, the top line is 7 8 9 and the third line is 1 2 3. On the phone, the top line is 1 2 3 and the third line is 7 8 9. 4 5 6 is on the second line on both and the zero is on the fourth line on both. There must be a reason for this. I once read a theory that said that the adding machine was in use first and that accountant types were very, very fast in punching in those numbers. When the phone panel went from dial to touch, the order of numbers was reversed from the calculator so that those very, very fast folks wouldn't dial (touch) the phone numbers too quickly and foul up the system. It could be true. Then came the TV remote control which is like the phone, 1 2 3 on top. Attention wives. The fact that the phone and the clicker are the same does not mean that you should ever touch the remote. The clicker, like MPB, is for husbands only.

I discovered a new law of physics while hanging Christmas tree ornaments this year. When first hung on the tree, the ornament will always face the wrong direction. This is like the rules that toast will always fall jelly side down and cats will always land on their feet. One scientist taped a piece of toast, jelly side up on the back of a cat and dropped it. Apparently the cat & the toast are still spinning in mid-air.

Have you tried to wrap something in Cling (it used to be called Saran Wrap) lately? The product is apparently being produced by psychiatrists to drum up business. It's nearly impossible to get it out of the box, then more impossible to tear it off on the bottom of the box and then it doesn't "cling" like it used to. It will drive you crazy. If psychiatrists are serious about food preservation, maybe they could come up with their own "Psychiatrist Cling" called "shrink-wrap".

I WOULD GUESS THAT THEY DON'T HAVE "SHOP" CLASSES IN HIGH SCHOOL ANY MORE. IF THEY DO, IT'S PROBABLY FOR FEMALE STUDENTS AND THEY MEET AT THE MALL.

I read recently that people who are born in the autumn live longer. At first I was confused because I couldn't think exactly when autumn is. I've got summer down pretty well, but the other seasons require thought. First of all, why do we have 5 names for 4 seasons? If summer is June, July and August, then March, April and May must be spring. December, January and February must be winter, so that leaves September, October and November as fall or autumn or both. Leaves fall in the fall, which makes it easier to remember, but did you ever see a leaf autumn?

So anyway, if you were born in September, October or November, a study of a million people in Germany says that you will live longer. About 6 months longer than those born in the spring. The guess is that pregnant women have better diets (more vitamins) if their last months of pregnancy are in the summer. This is useless information, of course, because if you are reading this, your birth date is pretty well already established. You might alter your birth certificate but, as we learned in a TV commercial several years ago, you can't fool Mother Nature and you could also have trouble running for President. So the only benefit this information has, is that you can plan to have your children born in the autumn, which means, if you don't want to do the math yourself, that the child should be conceived in December, January or February. Time is short. Take heed.

There are, it seems, dozens of charitable organizations in Waco that have great fund raising events. A Cattleman's Ball for cancer, Rockin Heart Ranch for hearts and a Margarita and Salsa party for arthritis. At any given time in the US, however, there are only so many people who suffer from each of these maladies. Maybe 10% have heart problems, 15% have arthritis and 8% have cancer? Who knows? But there is one serious problem that most all females and many males have at least occasionally. Sore feet. Women have more problems than men because they wear shoes specifically designed to create pain. Put men in high-heeled-pointed-toe shoes and that concept would last about two minutes. Anyway, I think we all need to get behind a fund-raiser to fight the sore feet crisis. I was thinking of a walk-a-thon.

Which came first," gig'em aggies", "hook'em horns" or "sic'em bears." And what exactly does "gig" mean? The dictionary offers many definitions of "gig": something that whirls, as in whirligig; a person of grotesque appearance; a rowboat designed for speed; a one horse carriage; a spear for catching fish (as in a frog gig); a job for a musician; and finally a military demerit. I would have guessed that the Aggie gig was the military demerit gig. I would have been wrong. The Aggies were playing the TCU Hornfrogs in 1930 and at yell practice a man named Pinky Downs said that the next day they would "Gig" the Hornfrogs and held up his thumb. This became the first hand sign and hand-sign-slogan in the Southwest Conference.
"Hook'em" wasn't begun until 1955 (created by UT cheerleader Harley Clark). "Sic'em was begun in 1960 by BU cheerleader Bobby Schrade, but wasn't officially sanctioned until 1972 while Baylor students and administrators debated as to whether it was "dignified" enough. I'm not sure how you quantify dignity as it relates to a hand sign. I guess you have to be an academic. Academically speaking, I think that the "hook 'em" sign looks more like a frog gig than the raised thumb. Maybe Pinky was really just going to hitchhike to TCU.

We went to the movies awhile back and arrived in time to see all of the previews. There are lots of previews. They preview movies that are 6 months off. The weird thing is that before every single movie preview, they put a disclaimer on the screen that says, "This preview has been approved

by the Motion Picture Association for all audiences." I kept waiting
for one that said, "This preview has not been approved for adults whose
intelligence is easily insulted, so if you are one, leave the theater for the
next 2 minutes".

This is like all bank ads having to say "Member FDIC". Why not
make just the ones (if there are any) who aren't a member of FDIC say so?

Remember that emordnilap is palindrome spelled backwards.

I recently found myself loitering in a drug store. For some reason
that I can't really explain, I started reading cans of hairspray. The
perceived holding power of hairspray is apparently a very important
selling point. There are no hairsprays that claim to be "Pretty Good" or
"Fairly Strong". No, hairsprays are a powerful force of nature. They start
with Firm Hold and then move on to Extra Hold, Super Hold, Extra Super
Hold, Super Firm Hold, Ultimate Hold, Ultra Firm Hold, Mega Hold,
Maximum Hold and the dreaded Freeze Hold. Why not just name them
Helmet Head or Concrete Hair?

I was thinking about coaches and what they wear to games. Football
coaches (with the exception of Tom Landry and a few others) wear casual
clothes. Pants, knit shirts or sweaters. Baseball coaches (who are called
managers as though coaching is beneath them) wear the same uniform as
their players. Basketball coaches dress like they're going to church instead
of the gym. I wonder how this came about? What if football coaches wore
football uniforms? Could Jimmy Johnson have gotten a helmet over his
hair? Would Mack Brown look good in shoulder pads? If basketball coaches
wore uniforms, how would Don Nelson look in shorts? Or if baseball
managers dressed like basketball coaches, how would Baylor Coach Steve
Smith look in an Armani suit walking to the pitcher's mound?

Some news items you know are true because you couldn't make them
up. A metroplex kid blinded himself by shooting himself in the face with
a live frog from a potato gun. You couldn't make that up. I'd never heard of
a "potato" gun (or "potatoe" gun as Dan Quayle might call it). Apparently
it's some sort of homemade gun using PCV pipe generally used to shoot
potatoes. I'm not sure why one would want to shoot a potato out of a gun,
or with a gun for that matter. What's a potato ever done to you? OK, there
is that cholesterol thing, but it's not personal. This young man apparently
tired of shooting potatoes and decided to shoot a live frog through the air.
The gun misfired and the young man looked into the wrong end of the gun

to see what was wrong and then it fired. This is a truly sad story. For the boy, for the frog and for the NPA (National Potato-Gun Association).

One of the major problems facing our country today is that we (or at least I) can't open packages. Manufacturers want you to buy their products, but they don't want you to use them. I bought some scissors for my office the other day but couldn't open the incredibly heavy industrial-strength-plastic package because... I didn't have any scissors. If I had had a hand grenade, I would have used it.

Speaking of scissors, do orange handled scissors cut better than other colors, or is it just my imagination?

I read that smokers are more likely to be allergic to earrings than non-smokers. Who figured this out? And how and why? I didn't know anybody was allergic to earrings. Smoking and earrings. Another crisis to create stress in the lives of Hell's Angels. Maybe it's a problem that will solve itself. Fewer people are wearing earrings anyway. They can't open the packages.

A MIDDLE AGE MAN WAS SEEN WEARING AN EARRING. WHEN ASKED HOW LONG HE'D BEEN WEARING IT, HE SAID SINCE HIS WIFE FOUND IT IN HIS CAR.

I was watching the news recently and saw some young men somewhere in the Middle East throwing rocks at an armored vehicle. What are they teaching these kids in school? Throwing a rock at a tank is like trying to teach a pig to sing. It just tires you out and irritates the pig.

VH1 (apparently an MTV for somewhat older teenagers) put out a list of the top 100 songs of the last 25 years a few weeks ago. Coming in at number one was a song by Nirvana that I'd never heard or heard of. (Remember, a preposition is a word that you should never end a sentence with.) It (the song, not the preposition) was titled "Smells Like Teen Spirit." I heard the song on a radio news report about its winning first place. It smells like something or other. This awards means one of two things. 1. I'm way too old. 2. There were no good songs in the last 25 years.

Of the top 20 on their list, five (I think) were in the rap arena. ("Rap Music" is an oxymoron.) Other "artists" included Def Leppard, Pink Floyd, The Police, Prince, Eminem, Dead Purple Horse, Public Enemy, No Doubt, TLC, R.E.M., Acid Reflux, AC/DC, Guns and Roses and Run-D.M.C. (I made up Dead Purple Horse and Acid Reflux just to see if you were paying attention, but there could be groups by those names, and I just haven't heard of them yet.)

You can be born or married at night, but can you be buried at night? I've never heard of a nighttime funeral. Why not? In July and August in Texas the heat at cemeteries during afternoon funerals can be enough to create the need for additional funerals. A nighttime funeral would be a relief (at least for the guests if not for the honoree). Folks wouldn't have to take off work. So why not have them? Is it because there are no lights at the cemetery? That could be remedied. I think it's a safety issue. At a night funeral, the cars in the funeral procession would have to drive with their lights off and that would create a traffic hazard.

I'm sure that at some time you've seen those height and weight charts, which say, for instance, that if you're a 50-year-old male who is six feet tall, you should weigh about 135 pounds. I don't know who comes up with those charts, but they don't live in the same world with the rest of us. Maybe they work for the government in California. Or France. Instead of encouraging you to quit eating, they encourage you to quit reading. (Speaking of France, a reader accused me of being a "Francophobe". That's impossible. No one [including Luxemburg] is afraid of France.)

But here's a suggested chart for your weight analysis. Weigh yourself while fully dressed as you prepare to leave for work. Make the following deductions. Shoes, 5 pounds. Socks and/or hose 2 pounds. Pants or skirt, 3 pounds. Shirt or blouse, 2 pounds. Suit coat, 4 pounds. Tie, 1 pound. Belt, one pound (2 pounds if over 40 inches). Hairspray, 2 pounds. Lipstick, 1 pound. Mascara, 1 pound. Eye shadow, 1 pound (if purple, 2 pounds). Earrings, 2 pounds. Necklace, 3 pounds. Watch, 1 pound. Wedding ring, women, 2 pounds, wedding ring, men, 2 ounces. Short hair, 3 pounds. Long hair, 5 pounds. Mustache or beard, 2 pounds. Fingernail polish, 1 pound. Black fingernail polish, 2 pounds. Thus, as an example, a woman with long hair, purple eye shadow and suit coat can deduct 33 pounds. (The same woman with a mustache can deduct 35 pounds.) You're welcome and have a nice day.

I got an important looking letter in the mail. (Why do we say "I got a letter in the mail"? Where else would we get a letter? In the refrigerator?) Anyway, the nice letter said that I had been nominated to be in Who's Who in America for 2003. I was getting kind of puffed up till I noticed that the nice letter was addressed to "Occupant". I think maybe occupant had a better year than I did.

It could be worse. I have a friend who says he keeps getting "pre-rejected" credit card offers. He gets those offers "in the mail".

I heard a Doctor of some sort saying that obesity should be classified as a disease. He said that obesity was caused by a "disregulation of eating". I'm more concerned about a "disregualtion of speaking". Exactly how does one "disregulate" one's eating. Maybe you don't get your food in the refrigerator, but "in the mail".

Am I the only one who gets confused when told to hit the "pound sign" or the "star" on the cell phone? To me, the "pound" sign is really a "number" sign (as in #3). The "star" sign is really an "asterisk". When told to hit the pound sign, I first think of hitting "lb" (as in 3 lbs). When told to hit the star sign, I can't find one. Maybe if we changed our state's nickname to the "Lone Asterisk State", I could keep it straight.

I heard that the average American throws away 4 pounds (4 #'s) of garbage a day. I think somebody else is throwing away garbage on my behalf. I'm not making my 4 pounds (4 #'s) a day share. Now if Vicki would just throw away all of the catalogs she gets, we could make our joint 8 pounds (8 #'s) a day easily.

It was reported that a Baylor toxicologist is studying antidepressants in the waterways and what effect this might have on fish. I guess it's like perch Prozac or bass Valium. Are fish depressed or just submerged? How much more laid back can a fish be? Fish stress? Another crisis of which I was unaware. How will we ever treat fish antidepressant addiction? They can't walk, so a "twelve-step" program is out. Maybe a "twelve-stroke" program? I heard years ago that the Aggie women's swim team had filed an official protest against the UT women after a Southwest Conference swim meet. They said the UT women were using their arms in the breaststroke competition. Turns out it wasn't true. It was just a joke.

Sometimes the same basic meal in a restaurant costs a couple of dollars more at night than it does at noon. Does this make since? Does the cost of food increase as the hours in the day increase? I would guess that their answer would be that the dinner has larger portions than the lunch. Why is that? Isn't it best to eat less at night? Shouldn't your largest meal of the day be at noon? Inquiring minds want to know.

The other day someone, in giving directions, said that A was kitty-cornered from B. It sounded odd to me. I think I say catty-cornered.

Is it kitty-cornered or catty-cornered? I looked it up and both are in the dictionary. Why? Is a catty-corner older than a kitty-corner? Will a kitty-corner eventually grow up to be a catty-corner? Do cats run across the street diagonally? How did this get started?

Another day, another strange scientific theory. I heard a report that, according to a "scientist," global warming is being caused by sooty snow. Apparently "sooty" snow just isn't as cold as the pure driven snow. Dirty snow creates higher temperatures, and that, Virginia, is why it's so hot in Texas in August. It could also be the increased use of sparklers on New Year's Eve. It could be the increased use of hair dryers. It could be Daylight Savings Time (that extra hour of sunlight has to hurt). It could be the large number of bald and balding men who have more heat escaping from their heads. Scientists recently said that coffee is good for you (in 6 months it will again be bad for you again), so it could be the extra coffee. It could be the hot air coming from scientists.

I was listening to a weatherman (male weatherperson) the other night and he discussed the weather "back east" and "out west." I wonder how the east got to be "back" and the west got to be "out." I guess it's because it would sound really stupid to say "out east" or "back west." "Up" north and "down" south make since, so we should probably say "left" west and "right" east.

A recent headline said, "FDA wants warning on anti-depressants". The story said that the FDA wanted anti-depressants to have a warning that if you take this medicine you might become suicidal. Gee, if you take an anti-depressant that makes you three times as depressed, maybe more than a warning label is needed. At least a stronger warning label, such as "Taking this pill may have the exact opposite effect it is intended to have. Unless your Doctor is Dr. Kevorkian, you might chose to avoid it" Duh!

I was driving on Highway 6 recently and was behind a huge tractor that was driving in the right lane, but not on the shoulder. I wondered why he didn't pull over. When I eventually passed him, I discovered that he was busy. He was talking on the phone. For some reason it seemed strange. Driving a tractor and talking on the phone just didn't compute. Of course, plowing and tractors have changed. This plow person was in a glass enclosed, air-conditioned compartment, no doubt with a killer sound system. Farmers, while plowing, used to worry about grasshoppers and sunburn. Now I guess they worry about woofers and tweeters and being in a "good cell".

Gay marriage is sparking national debate these days. There are some potential problems with some "you know what" marriages that may not have yet been contemplated. Like who gets their picture in the paper? We all know that only the bride can have "her" picture in the paper. If "Adam and Eve" become "Adam and Steve" or "Madam and Eve" who gets a picture on the bridal page? Do you believe in gay divorce?

Once a year you have to buy an inspection sticker for your car. If your sticker runs out in September, wait till the first of October to get the new one. By adding a month each year, in only 12 years you can save $10.50. Of course you do have to keep the same car for 12 years, but for $10.50, you might consider it.

I recently had a conversation with a local big shot business executive. (Would it narrow it down too far if I said she was a bank president?) She was commenting and complaining about how large her home's water bill was. I asked if she had an automatic sprinkler system. She said yes. I asked if she had a pool. She said yes. But, she said, it wasn't the pool or the sprinkler system that was using too much water, it was her husband who let the water run the entire time he was brushing his teeth instead of cutting the water on and off as needed. So there. With proper husband-water-use-training (HWUT) you can probably cut your water bill in half. Husbands! Of course it's his fault. As has been asked, if a husband says something in the middle of a forest and no one hears him, is he still wrong?

I was watching some politically correct TV program (the Democrat convention, I think) and noticed that instead of saying "men and women" folks were saying "women and men". It's OK, it just sounds odd. To be fair (fair and balanced) they should also say "Gentlemen and Ladies".

I was surprised recently to open a Chinese fortune cookie and find the fortune printed in English and Spanish. Those Chinese factory workers have gone from bi-lingual to tri-lingual. Smart cookies. I'm monolingual. I took Latin in high school and college. That was a really smart move. If I ever run into ancient Roman, I can tell him that "All Gaul was divided into three parts".

Anyone younger than 50 and who didn't take Latin has no idea what I'm talking about. There are many things that our children don't know about and most of it is good. For instance...what it means to defrost a refrigerator...how to use a slide rule or do math with a pencil and paper... how to warm food without a microwave... how to play baseball with no adults around... how to play solitaire with real cards... how to use a pay phone... how to hand-write a letter.

NEWS BULLETIN. SCIENTIST NOW REPORT THAT THERE IS A SUCKER BORN EVERY 54 SECONDS.

As one with a beard, I might point out that of the seven dwarves, only Dopey had a clean-shaven face.

I don't watch wrestling (rasslin) on television, but I don't mean to denigrate those who do. And for the people who do watch rasslin on TV, denigrate means to put down.

Happy New Year. It's great to have a holiday that you can mention without the chance of offending someone. But who knows. There could be a cult of very sensitive Old-Yearians out there somewhere.

When Vicki and I were first married, we lived in a small duplex in Austin in which the bedroom was a loft kind-of-a-deal. The stairs to the loft had a landing in the middle and Vicki (an inveterate decorator) put some sort of decoration in the corner of the landing. One day, soon after we had moved in, she came home with a load of groceries. Included was a can of spinach. Partly in jest, and partly in self-preservation, I hid the can of spinach behind the decoration on the stairs. I soon forgot about it and Vicki never knew about it until we moved out of the duplex months later and she found the hidden can of spinach. I can't remember if she saw the humor, but at least I had avoided the vile taste of cooked spinach.

I thought about this because there was an item in the news about a scientist at M.I.T. who has developed a system to use spinach (the energy that spinach uses during photosynthesis to convert light to energy) to extend the life of batteries, like those in cell phones. Spinach was chosen because it has a lot of chlorophyll, is cheap and readily available. This is thrilling news. An actual viable use for spinach. I suggest that we all stop eating spinach so that there will be plenty for science. I know that I'm going to do my part. I will also never again eat a cell phone battery.

Did you hear about the Texas woman who paid $50,000 for a cloned cat. The name of the California cloning company is actually "Genetics Savings and Clone." You couldn't make that up. I've always admired cloners with a sense of humor. Anyway, if you are desperate to have a pet very, very, very similar to your former pet, just call or write my new company "Ice Cream Clone." Send a picture of the dearly departed and we will find a very, very, very similar replacement. There is currently a half price special. Your new cat will only cost $25,000. You're welcome.

You may have seen that last month would have been Elvis's 70th birthday. (For those of you who think he's still alive, it was his 70th birthday.) Don't you wish he were still around to see how he would be at 70? Could he still shake an artificial hip? There might be new words to "Heartbreak Hotel"... such as... "Since my wife has passed (Bum Bum)... I've found a new place eat (Bum Bum)...It's down at the end of lonely street... at Golden Years Retreat... (Bum Bum Bum) I feela so dizzy baby. I feela so dizzy baby... I feela so dizzy... I could fall."

It's been said that, "Everyone talks about the weather, but no one does anything about it." The last couple of months have been a little strange temperature-wise. One day it's cold, then warm, then cool, then rainy. You really have to watch the weatherman (male weatherperson) at night to know how to dress the next day. Which brings up an interesting point. I work, or at least my office is in, the very nice ALICO building. The temperature in my office is the same year around, which is a cool 68 to 70 degrees. In the summer, I might wear a short sleeve shirt. In the winter a long sleeve shirt and a sweater. The temperature in the office is always the same, but my attire is entirely different. Apparently my body adjusts without even thinking about it. So who cares? I guess it wasn't really an interesting point after all. Never mind.

Remember, no matter what the temperature of the room is, it's always room temperature.

Speaking of weatherpersons, a Texas legislator introduced a bill to make it a crime for a weatherperson to be called a "meteorologist" unless he or she has a four-year degree in Meteorology. The legislator's thought process (or lack thereof) was that a weatherperson, who claims to be a meteorologist, but isn't, might give a bad forecast and someone might believe it and somehow endanger himself because of it and he wouldn't have believed it if he didn't think that the weatherperson was a "real" meteorologist. (That sentence was as difficult to write, as it is to read.) Apparently the legislator believes that somewhere, somebody actually believes a weather forecast. This isn't true. The purpose of weather forecasters is to make economists look good. Besides, the only school in Texas that offers a degree in Meteorology is Texas A&M. Some people don't want to be meteorologists...some people don't want to be Aggies...but some do want to be both.

A recent study indicated that the less you sleep, the more weight you gain and vice versa. I guess that you have to have a certain amount of sleep for your body to metabolize whatever it is trying to metabolize. Another study says that thinner people live longer. Another study said that people who go to church live longer. Maybe there's a grand correlation with these studies. That extra 15 minutes of sleep that people get in church, makes them thinner and therefore able to live longer. Boiling all of these studies down, if you want to live longer...sleep in church. Don't, however, stay after church for the potluck lunch.

My church can prove that churchgoers live longer. The average age of my congregation is about 78 and I'm considered a youngster. That's another benefit to going to church. You can look around and feel young.

Since I am less young, I take more pills. Vicki got me one of those plastic things that has a compartment for each day's pills. It works great. Before, I had no idea how many days I had forgotten to take my pills.

Sometimes it seems that all that Doctors do these days is prescribe pills. No matter what problem you have, there is a pill for it. You meet with the Doc for four minutes and get five prescriptions.

We all know that there is a crisis in this country with the high and increasing cost of healthcare. There are small emergency clinics that have been referred to as a "Doc in a Box". Perhaps we should take this one step farther and have a "Drive-Thru-Doc-In-a-Box". You would drive up to a menu board with a list of symptoms. The unseen nurse on the inside with the headphones would say, "Can I take your order?" You'd say, "Well, I guess I have a...uh...headache...and a runny nose...and a...uh, cough." The nurse would say, "Is that a small cough or a regular cough?" You'd say 'Oh, I guess a small cough." The nurse would say, "OK. That's a number 3, a number 5 and a small number 8. Do you want hives with that?" You'd say, "No thanks." She'd say, "OK, that will be $162.50. Drive up to the 2nd window". When you pull up to window number two, you'd get three prescriptions and a happy toy. You wouldn't have to see a doctor or a real human being at all. Think of the money that could be saved.

A friend was telling a story about a problem caused by missing an exit on the freeway because he was too deep in thought. That is not my problem. Most of my problems have been caused because I was too shallow in thought.

I didn't think my "Turn Your Headlights On for the Outlawing of Neckties" campaign would catch on so quickly in Waco, but by 10 p.m., everyone in town was promoting it.

They say, "Don't snack between meals." When do they think we should snack? During meals? I tried it. It just doesn't work.

I was reading something recently that said that so-and-so had "egg on his face." I know what it means, but why "egg"? I got to thinking, when was the last time I had egg on my face? I don't eat eggs that often, but I can't remember the last time I got some on my face or why. Maybe we need a new expression. How about "so-and-so had barbeque sauce on his face?" That works for me. Often.

My car will get an average of 400 miles per tank of gas. However, when the gauge shows half full, it's already gone 300 miles. Why, according to the gauge, does that last half of a tank of gas only go about a third of the first half? At first, I thought it was just my car, but now I'm in the third car that does this. What's wrong with gas gauges? Do they have barbeque sauce on their faces?

While it is probably an embarrassment to Baylor, it is true, nonetheless, that I taught a class there for two semesters a few years ago. The dean of the school in which I taught is a very nice man. (I'm sucking up in case there is another opportunity some day.) When we discussed my employment at Thee University, he explained that I needed to submit a statement about my religious status. The main question was whether or not I was a Christian. My answer was...that I was pretty close. I was Presbyterian.

We Presbyterians can't really be considered "real" Christians because we missed out on the whole Juswanna phenomenon. Juswanna, as you know, has dominated "real" Christian prayer for many years now. Apparently Presbyterians were home sick the day they taught Juswanna at prayer school. You know what I mean, "We juswanna thank you Lord", "We juswanna praise you Lord", "We juswanna ask you Lord...." Presbyterians juswanna ask for forgiveness for missing the whole juswanna deal. (My spell checker wants me to change "juswanna" to "hosanna". It that weird or what? Is my spell checker afraid that "juswanna" might be sacrilegious?)

Did I ever mention that I can't eat burned toast? It's a medical problem. I'm "black toast intolerant." (I report. You deride.)

I figured out why the folks at the garden store call that stuff "potting soil." It's because if they called it a "bag of dirt," nobody would buy it. Not at that price.

I watched replay highlights of the Senate Hearings for the Supreme Court judgeship. They should change the name of Senate Hearings to Senate Talkings. There was no hearing, just talking. If I had been on the committee, I would have voted against Judge Roberts. Not for his judicial philosophy, but because of his movie choices. He said his favorite all-time movies were Dr. Zhivago and North By Northwest. I don't really remember if I ever saw North By Northwest, but it was probably a great movie. I only remember that it was an Alfred Hitchcock movie and that Gary Grant was chased across a field by a deranged crop duster or some such.

However, whenever I'm asked what was the worst movie that I ever saw was, I always say Dr. Zhivago. The only way it could have been worse was for it to have lasted longer, and it lasted about a week. (Google is a wonderful thing. I looked it up and Dr. Zhivago was 3 hours and 17 minutes. It seemed much longer.) The movie won 5 Oscars in 1965 (Art Direction, Score, Costumes, Screenplay, Cinematography) but not Best Picture or Best Director. The Sound of Music won both of those. Dr. Zhivago was as boring as a drill press. If my math is correct, Chief Justice John Roberts was only 10 years old when Dr. Z was released, so maybe he never saw it. He was 4 years old when North by Northwest was released. He must like watching old movies.

From the big screen to the little screen. If your plasma screen television needed a transfusion, would you order a Direct IV? Would your HBO cover it?

I saw a headline that said: "Indian Chef Currying Favor with British". That's a clever use of the word "currying" when referring to Indian food that uses an inordinate amount of the foul tasting spice called curry. (If I think curry is foul tasting, should I think chicken is "fowl tasting"?) Anyway, this isn't really about curry, but about the Indian Chef. My eye saw "Indian Chef", but my mind read "Indian Chief". I was having a hard time figuring out what an Indian Chief was doing in England. Were the redskins and the red coats getting back together? Can you not say "redskins" unless you play football in DC? Why isn't DC PC?

I remember when the Washington Bullets, a District of Columbia NBA basketball team, changed their name to avoid being associated with crime. They changed their name from the Washington Bullets to just... The Bullets.

Speaking of sports, the wife of a friend said that she got mad every time she went bowling. I think she might have Irritable Bowl Syndrome. (I'm just the messenger. Don't strike me; spare me.)

I was watching an NFL game when some big bruiser got penalized for "tripping." Let's see. It's OK to pick up a player and throw him to the ground like a rag doll, or run 20 miles and hour and hit him in the stomach with your helmet... but it's a penalty to trip him? What? Afraid he'll fall down?

I don't like to think too deeply, but I think that if I could go back and live my life all over again, I'd part my hair on the other side.

Here are a couple of handy hints for around the house this fall. If you're going to burn your leaves, rake them into a pile first. It will save a lot of time and matches. And for your holiday cooking you should be aware that if the recipe calls for "allspice", "Old Spice" just won't work. Trust me.

Speaking of cooking, a local restaurant, Buzzard Billy's, offers alligator on its menu. I wonder if they can cook it in a crock-pot?

I saw a bumper sticker that said, "Don't honk if you can't read this." I didn't know what to do... or not do. I did nothing, but that might have been wrong.

The end of December was the 1st year anniversary of the terrible Asian Tsunami. I heard a news report that said, "220,000 people were killed, many of whom were women and children". Well, let's see. A little more than half of the world's population is female and probably 20% are children, so yeah, many of them were women and children. The question is why do we always report that women and children were among the victims? Are men completely worthless? Whenever there is a plane crash, it is reported that "women and children were among the victims". You can just hear the "good" news someday; "A tornado struck an Oklahoma trailer park today. There were at least 100 victims. Thank God, only men died." Of course it's always "Women and children in the lifeboats first"? How did men get to be so expendable? Who do I call?

I hear a radio ad for a product called HeightMax. It's a pill for kids (actually it's a pill for parents) who aren't as tall as their parents think they ought to be. These folks advertise that by taking this pill, your son or daughter can add up to three additional inches in height (and no doubt become a college basketball star). I would like to get a list of every parent who buys this pill. I want to sell them another pill called SmartMax. SmartMax would keep you from throwing your money away on really dumb ideas.

IS THERE EVER A DAY IN THE YEAR THAT MATTRESSES ARE NOT ON SALE? JUST WONDERING.

One day I was in a big hurry and my low-fuel light came on. So I pulled into a station and quickly got $5 worth of gas. When I drove off my low fuel light was still on.

One of the things that they say separates us humanoids from animals is the "opposable thumb". My thumbs, by the way, are very easygoing and not really opposed to anything. But I guess the "opposable thumb" allows us to grab things that horses, dogs and goats can't grab. (Cats can probably grab them if you're not looking.) Being able to "grab things" has thus made us superior. Who knew? Anyway, I was thinking of thumbs the other day (it was a very slow day) and I'll bet that thumbs have been used more since cell phones were invented than in all previous recorded history combined.

I'm thinking of having my cell phone "ring" changed to a loud sneeze. That way, not only will I not offend those around me, they might bless me when my phone rings.

You don't have to answer this, but what if there were no hypothetical questions?

Are we having the "Revenge of the Creatures"? The news is full of dire warnings of Bird Flu and Mad Cow Disease. Have we irritated the animal kingdom? I have to admit that many years ago I used to go dove hunting, but I've never harmed a cow. I apologize for the one out of twenty doves that I shot at and hit. It was nothing personal (or birdal). Let's hope that grackles don't get mad at us or we'll all be doomed.

I don't know why people complain about high long-distance phone rates. I can pick up a phone right now and talk to someone in India for free.

You've probably seen the billboards that say, "We buy ugly houses". Is this something to be proud of? If you bought an ugly house, would you be bragging? If you buy ugly clothes, would you want to advertise it to the masses? Maybe there could be a big bumper sticker that says, "I Bought an Ugly Car". If you do something that is aesthetically displeasing, don't brag about it. We'll know. You won't have to tell us.

Would it be funny if you called the We Buy Ugly House folks and told them you were one of your friends or neighbors and wanted to sell your house? Would you want to be there when the Ugly House person showed up?

I sometimes enjoy using self-deprecating humor... but I'm not very good at it.

Here's some good advice that you might try. If you're suffering from stress and tension and you get a headache, do what it says on the aspirin bottle. "Take two aspirin" and "Keep away from children."

YOU KNOW WHAT SEEMS ODD TO ME? NUMBERS THAT AREN'T DIVISIBLE BY TWO.

I recently heard someone say that people were buying something "like it was going out of style." If something's going out of style, why would you want to buy it? Like, it's going to be out-of-style, Dude.

Texas is, of course, unique. Just like every other state. But, I would argue, we are more unique. (Some grammarians would argue that something can't be "more" unique. It's either unique or it's not. To heck with them!) We have official "things" that I bet other states don't have. You know about the State Flower (Bluebonnet,) the State Bird (Mockingbird) and the State Song (Texas Our Texas.) Did you know we have three state mammals? We have a large mammal (Longhorn,) a small mammal (Armadillo) and a flying mammal (the Mexican Free-tailed Bat.)

I'm wondering who lobbied for the Mexican Free-tailed Bat? Is there a large group of weird bat supporters out there? Are they batty? Do they hang from the ceiling? Why do we have more mammals than any other category? There's only one State Insect (the Monarch Butterfly). The weirdest category of all, however, is the official State Dinosaur (the Brachiosaur Sauropod, Pleurocoelus). If you see one of those in Texas, you may be batty.

I once saw a sign in an office in the Texas Capitol that said, "If it ain't broke... fix it till it is!" Words to live by. (Or if that same grammarian is still around... Words by which to live.)

OK. So some smart aleck group of scientists (The International Astronomical Union) got together and decided that Pluto was too little to be a "real" planet. Oh yeah! Well so's your mother (too little to be a planet). If Pluto was big enough to be a planet in my elementary school science book, it's big enough today. This group is obviously afflicted with "sizeism" and therefore probably racism, sexism, ageism and they probably don't like greasy hamburgers and french fries and second helpings of Blue Bell homemade vanilla. In reference to the Pluto decision, I think this is a Mickey Mouse organization and that they are all Goofy.

To add insult to injury, they have renamed Pluto by giving it an asteroid number, #134340. This was done by the Minor Planet Center. How would you like to work at the Minor Planet Center? There's a great resume enhancer.

I read that a driver from Switzerland was caught doing a hundred in a sixty mile-per-hour zone on a highway in eastern Ontario, Canada. His excuse? " He said he was taking advantage "of the ability to go faster without risking hitting a goat." So if the DPS really wants Texas drivers to slow down, it's easy. Just put some goats on the highways. It works great in Switzerland.

Now that the spinach scare is over and the lettuce scare is over... what's next? Carrots? Did Popeye survive the spinach crisis? If they can do away with Pluto, they can do away with Popeye. I haven't seen Popeye lately and I'm getting worried.

Have you noticed that in the last few years the media and scientists and government health people seem to be constantly trying to scare us half-to-death? (What happens if you're scared half-to-death twice?) There was SARS (whatever that was) and the bird-flu and the avian flu and just plain flu and mad-cow disease and melting ice caps and God knows what-all. Something was going to kill us every month. Like Flower-of-the-Month we've had a Pandemic-of-the-Month. So far it's all been unnecessary hype.

You just can't let everything scare you. Are you losing sleep over North Korean nukes? Iranian nukes? (Can you say Iranian Uranium fast three times?) Worried about Islamofacist? Well I've never met anyone from Islam. I can't even find it on a map.

Speaking of sleeping, do you ever get a great idea in the middle of the night, then the next day you remember that you had a great idea but can't remember what it was? Well, last night, in the middle of the night, I thought of a great way to save those ideas. All you do is... um... er... oh heck... never mind.

I was looking at some church choir music. The last page of the music said, "This page was intentionally left blank." Well, it would have been blank if it hadn't had that sentence in the middle of the page, which said, "This page was intentionally left blank."

Can you tell if your email is from a man or woman? Does email have a recognizable gender? If so should we call it hemail and shemail? Or femail?

My orange juice bottle said it was 100% orange juice... from concentrate. What does that mean? Where is Concentrate? I thought orange juice came from Florida. If it's 100% orange juice why did it have to be concentrated? I can't think about this any more; I've lost my power of concentration.

We had an interesting procession of funerals (as opposed to a funeral procession) recently. In the same week Saddam, Gerald Ford and James Brown died. President Ford died at the end of a lengthy illness. Saddam died at the end of a lengthy rope. I guess the "Hardest Working Man in Show business" died from working too hard. I got to see a James Brown concert back in the 60's and he was amazingly entertaining. I have no idea how someone can scream that much and keep his voice. He could dance better than Gerald and Saddam put together, although Saddam did have that dancing at the end of a rope thing down.

I don't understand a lot of today's fashion. I see young men wearing sweatshirts and jackets on the top and shorts on the bottom. What's with these people? Does only the top half of their body get cold?

Driving down (that means going South) I-35 recently, I came upon a bumper sticker that said "RAISE CLAMS." I had to get closer to read the bottom line, which said "Not Sub-Divisions." This confused me. I didn't even know you could raise a clam, if you wanted to. Do they have little clam day schools? Do they have an Adopt-A-Clam program? And what's wrong with sub-divisions? I bet the sub-division people wish that the bumper sticker people would clam-up. Maybe they could compromise and create little sub-divisions just for clams. Anyway, I then looked at the license plate and the car was from Vermont. No doubt a snowbird enjoying our snow-free society and bringing news of the Great Vermont Clam Controversy to Texas.

Quick. Who has more people? McLennan County (of which Waco is the county seat) or Vermont? There are more than 200,000 folks in our fair county and the entire state of Vermont has a population of 146,000 people if you count the snowbirds, but not the clams. The largest town in Vermont? Burlington, with 39,000 people.

Speaking of driving down (or up) I-35, some people are not very good drivers. I call these people "Everybody but me".

And new gadgets are definitely for young folks. A friend, my age, got a new cell phone. It's very complicated. The first time he used it, he ended up playing "Hey Jude" and taking a picture of his ear.

Roger Kahn wrote a book about baseball called "The Boys of Summer". Baylor's first home baseball game was played on February 13th and the wind-chill temperature was in the 20's. I'm sure the players were numb. Maybe they were The Boys of Number.

WHAT DO YOU CALL A WIFE WHO KNOWS WHERE HER HUSBAND IS AT ALL TIMES? A WIDOW.

Remember, a wife lasts as long as the marriage does, but an ex-wife is forever.

Why are married women heavier than single women? Single women come home, see what's in the fridge and go to bed. Married women come home, see what's in the bed and go to the fridge.

There was a recent wedding picture in the newspaper that showed both the bride and groom, which is unusual in itself. But what really stood out was that the groom had a blue-tooth phone thingy in his ear. You know, this wedding picture is important and all, but hey, I could miss a call. Of course it might ring during the wedding ceremony. "Hold on there Preach, this could be important." Maybe that's why men aren't usually allowed in wedding pictures.

A few years ago, an aunt gave us a sundial for our garden. It's pretty neat if you can get it lined up right. A friend was visiting and asked what it was. I showed him how it worked & he said, "What won't they think of next!"

If my writing skills improve, I might look into getting Microsoft Sentence.

Am I getting older or are they playing better music in elevators and grocery stores?

Speaking of old, I read that scissors were invented around 1500 BC and paper was invented around 100 BC. I bet that before that, it was really boring playing Rock, Rock, Rock.

I have recently learned of something new that I am that I didn't know I was, or at least I didn't know there was a name for it. I am a "meatiest." or one guilty of "meatism." I learned this in a letter to the editor that said that "meatism is the single largest cause of environmental problems (not to mention health, societal and spiritual problems)" and in fact, "meatism is causing all of our problems..." Wow! Who knew? The letter writer, from Florida, calls himself "The Vegan Sage". I guess that a "sage" is a good thing for a vegan to be, cause it is both a philosopher and a plant. Vegans are vegetarians on steroids (organic, farm raised steroids). They not only don't eat meat, but they won't drink milk or eat cheese or even wear leather shoes. (I guess they wouldn't eat leather shoes either.) I don't know if vegans eat nuts, but they are nuts. But then it could be that meatism has ruined my thought processes. I'll ponder that over my next hamburger.

I MIGHT COULD TRY BEING A VEGETARIAN, ONCE REMOVED. I WOULD ONLY EAT ANIMALS THAT ONLY ATE VEGETABLES.

You may have noticed that we've had a lot of rain this year. Before I went to college (at The University) I had never seen a male person with an umbrella. I'm not sure if men, back then, were allowed to carry umbrellas in Falls County. Sheriff Pamplin may have outlawed it. The first time I saw a guy on campus carrying an umbrella, I thought that he must be the biggest sissy on earth. I couldn't believe it. Then, a short while later, after walking about a half mile from class back to my dorm room in a hard rain, I decided that I might ought to look into one of those sissy umbrella deals.

I've been carrying them ever since. Many restaurants, through the years, have benefited from my donations of umbrellas that I forgot that I had with me. Fortunately, they're not too expensive. I keep a spare in my trunk. A tire and an umbrella.

When you think of Britney, Paris and Lindsey (and it's hard to avoid sometimes) does the word "Celebretards" ever cross your mind? Celebrehab? Celebrelapse? Celebrepulse?

I attended a great night of music last month. It's an annual reunion of mostly jazz musicians who used to play together back in the 50's or so. These old guys (most are older than me) can still really play and the fun that they have is contagious. While there, I renewed an acquaintance with a young lady I worked with years ago, who had her four sons with her to hear their grandfather play the trumpet. The four boys were not only great looking kids, but were very well behaved. When I commented on their excellent decorum, she shared one of her disciplining secrets with me. She said that she once found this very feminine, small, frilly, pink purse made for little girls. She bought it and takes it with her when the boys are out in public. She assures the boys that if one of them acts badly, he will have to carry the purse. What a great idea. I imagine that feminists might object because they would want little boys to feel comfortable carrying a purse, but, thank God, most little boys are still boys. I think this "fear of public embarrassment" technique would also work with little girls. If they act badly, make them carry a frog.

You probably have read that some researcher said that being overweight is contagious. You can get it from your friends. The study said, and I'm not making this up, that people who hang out with overweight people become overweight themselves. I'm not sure if the reverse is true, but I'm thinking of starting a new business of supplying thin people for other people to hang out with. It would be a "Rent-A-Thin-Friend". The problem will be finding thin folks to rent out. The world is getting so overweight that I heard about a 250 pound anorexic.

Sometimes when driving down a country road at night, I wish I could turn off one headlight on my car and make people think I'm a motorcycle. But I can't, so I leave both headlights on and make 'em think I'm two motorcycles.

Why do we seem to always be short on math teachers? Can't they multiply?

A recent newspaper headline said "Acute Hospital Planned". It would have been less accurate, but more interesting if the headline had said "A Cute Hospital Planned". I'd much rather go to a "cute" hospital.

I imagine that a job as a ski-lift operator doesn't pay much, but is it's probably a great way to pick up women.

I recently saw some old friends, a retired couple, who eat out a lot. As a matter of fact, the husband said that they eat out so much that they are thinking of selling their kitchen. Well, if you can have a garage sale, why not a kitchen sale?

This is a family magazine and while it is not necessarily my goal to be "delicate", it is my goal to not be "indelicate". Anyway, there are many subjects about which it is very difficult to discuss and while doing so to maintain good taste. One was an incident last month in which a semi-public person was arrested in a local bar for conduct unbecoming a human being. It is difficult to discuss what he did, but let's just say that the other people in the bar were not as relieved as he was. I imagine that the incident will be resolved quickly in the legal system. On the other hand, the accused could demand a jury trial. If so, he could demand a jury of his pee-ers.

The New Year is a good time to look at our lives, evaluate our situation and think about what's really important. For instance, what if the hokey pokey really is what it's all about?

But who cares? I think the older I get, the more apathetic I'm becoming. For instance: Jimmy cracked corn and I don't care.

Even though today is the first day of the rest of my life, I think I'm gonna do pretty much the same stuff I did yesterday.

Did you hear about the actor Wesley Snipes being in trouble with the IRS? It seems that he made $38 million dollars over a five-year period and paid no income taxes at all. His excuse was that he earned his money by performing a service and not by producing a product and that only products were taxable. He said that his tax advisor convinced him that he was on good legal ground. His tax advisor, by the way, is in prison and on shaky ground, or actually a concrete floor. I wonder if Wesley likes prison movies?

There were several folks in Stephenville, Texas who recently saw a UFO. Ordinarily, I might scoff at this and ponder on drunken rednecks and their wild imaginations except for the fact that I recently saw a UFO also. No kidding. I was driving South on highway 6, near Marlin, and saw a brighter than normal light in the sky. It looked like a really bright star, but then I noticed that it was moving. As an old pilot, I watched it closely to determine if it was a plane or a helicopter. As I was watching it closely, it broke into two white pieces and the piece on the left showed a red light in the middle and then they both just instantly disappeared. I don't drink and my neck was it's normal color, moderately reddish. My first thought was that I might later hear about a plane crash, but I didn't. I have absolutely no idea what it was. Maybe I should start drinking. There are folks in Marlin who seem to be from outer space, so I guess it could have been a drop-off. Speaking of UFO and unusual happenings, have you noticed how many weird conspiracy theorists there are out there? What's the deal with that? Could it be Government Cloning Farms?

There is a product or institution called American Girl Dolls. They are apparently a big deal for little girls with generous parents. Somewhere in the greater Dallas area there is an American Girl Doll store, one of only a few in the USA. In that store is a hair salon where you can get your doll's hair fixed for only $20. Not your hair, but your doll's hair. I can get my hair fixed for $10, but the relatively small doll probably has more hair than I do. But why have fun when you can pay someone else $20 to have fun for you? What's all this talk about the terrible economy?

They say "money talks". Mine doesn't. It just goes without saying.

There was an actual news headline recently that said, "Texas Magician Charged after Girl Disappears from School." This was not a joke or even a human-interest story, it was a serious story about a kidnapping and fortunately the little girl was recovered unharmed. But hey, if every magician were arrested every time they made somebody disappear, we wouldn't have too many magic shows. And where is PETA when David Copperfield makes an elephant disappear? And where is the elephant?

A recent study reported that the average American golfer walks about 900 miles a year. Another study found American golfers drink, on average, 22 gallons of alcohol a year. Kind of makes you proud, doesn't it. Cause that means, on average, American golfers are getting about 41 miles to the gallon.

Did you hear the latest business news? It is rumored that Xerox and Wurlitzer might merge. If they do, they will manufacture reproductive organs.

Why, when I stop at the drive-thru at the bank, do I sometimes unbuckle my seat belt? Could it be dementia? It's possible. The other day, I got to my office door, took out my keys and pushed the car door opener to open the office door. It didn't work. But maybe that's an opportunity for you entrepreneurs out there. Include on the car door opener thingy, another button that will open your office or house door. I just want a small percent of the vast profits.

Another idea for you entrepreneurs. Given most peoples' attitudes in the morning, you might be able to hit it big with a cereal called "Grumpios."

Old age is tough. And how old do you have to be to die of old age? Personally, I intend to live forever...and so far, so good. Did you hear about the man who asked his Doctor what he had...and the Doctor said, "Natural Causes?"

I heard about a person of age (about my age) who was having a problem with his computer. He asked his teenage neighbor to help him. The teenager fixed the problem with a couple of quick keystrokes. The aged one asked what the problem was and the teenager said it was the normal ID Ten T problem. The man asked what the ID Ten T problem was and the young whippersnapper told him to write it down. So he did. ID10T.

Some alleged scientists in London have reported that obesity contributes to global warming. (As with all global warming, it must be George Bush's fault. He is probably secretly requiring the world to supersize its fries, which adds to heat and weight.) My first thought about global warming and fat people was that they sweat too much, but the scientists said that because they eat more, obese folks require more trucks to carry the additional food to the grocery stores and more food to be grown and besides that they drive more and walk less than thin people do. These scientists should spend their time on more significant studies, such as how to make powdered water. Does their study of obesity and global warming have the opportunity to have real significance? Fat chance! If it were true, however, one major advantage would be that Al Gore would have to go on a diet.

There's been a lot of talk about whether or not we should subject terror suspects to waterboarding. If the anti-waterboarding side wins, maybe we could subject terror suspects to snowboarding. It looks pretty dangerous to me. Or better yet, how about ironingboarding? Make them iron clothes until they talk. It would work for me.

I'm sure you've noticed that on the back of many men's blue jeans, such as Levis, the waist and leg-length size are printed on the little brown leather square right there on the back of the jeans where everybody in the world or in the elevator can see it. I imagine that you've also noticed that this is not done for women's jeans. How many pairs of women's jeans do you think would be sold if the waist size were printed right there for everyone to see? Maybe none?

Some enterprising jean maker ought to try putting the waist size on women's jeans, but they should put the size about 6 inches less than the actual size. That might sell.

Medical news to confuse. Breast self-exams can be dangerous. Sunscreen can be dangerous. Cell phones can be dangerous. Plastic water bottles can be dangerous. Tomatoes can be dangerous. Peppers can be dangerous. Taking medicine can be dangerous. Not taking medicine can be dangerous. Who knows what to do? Maybe quit reading?

Another sign that I'm getting older. I heard a really great old-time-rock-and-roll song on the radio and it made me want to play my air guitar. I wanted to play it, but I couldn't remember where I put it.

Former trial lawyer and former Vice Presidential candidate and would-be-president John Edwards said that when he had his extra-marital affair that his cancer-plagued wife was "in remission". So, I guess that made it all OK. Can't you just see Joe Sixpack (or Charlie Chardonnay) saying to his wife, "Well, I know I cheated on you, but it's OK cause you didn't have cancer". And then he could watch as she loaded the moving van or the gun.

Did you ever wonder how different things might be if all humans had evolved with purple skin? Neither did I.

Do you remember William Tell? He was famous for shooting an arrow into an apple, that was on top of someone's head,...and then I guess he later wrote the William Tell Overture. (Actually the William Tell Overture was written by someone named Rossini who was a big Lone Ranger fan.) Anyway, it is not as well known that William Tell and his whole family were ardent bowlers and very good at it. Unfortunately, however, all the league records from that time were destroyed in a fire. Thus we'll never know for whom the Tells bowled.

If you're still in the New Year's Resolution weight loss mode, you might try the Government Spending Diet. On the Government Spending Diet, if you slow the rate at which you gain, it counts as weight loss.

Most all of the news these days (Can you have "most all" of something? Wouldn't it either be all or not?) is about the sorry state of the economy. Things are bad, but could be worse. We could have invested our money with that guy Bernie Madoff. It's amazing how many smart people he swindled out of money. His method is called a "Ponzi Scheme," where he would pay off early investors with their own money and money from later investors and never really invest the money in anything...just keep getting new investors to give greater sums of cash to pay older investors and put a lot of it in his own pocket. Do you wonder how he came up with plan? I think he may have once worked for the Social Security Administration.

You probably saw that a 10-year old dog named Stump won the Best of Show at the Westminster dog show. Stump, a Texas dog that was once near death until saved by vets at Texas A&M, retired from the dog show biz a few years ago, but came out of retirement just in time for this year's big show. Stump is the oldest dog (70 in dog years) to ever win the BOS award and probably also has the most red-neckish name ever. A dog named Stump should be in a trailer park in West Texas, not in Westminster. A dog named Stump winning Westminster is like Lyle Lovett marrying Julia Roberts. There's hope for us all.

I stopped at a convenience store in Salado while coming back from Austin last month. The two young girl clerks behind the counter were talking and one of them was telling the story of how at her recent wedding, just as the couple were saying their "I Do's", the preacher's cell phone, in his coat pocket, began ringing. The preacher had on a lapel microphone, so it was really loud. For some reason, this really cracked me up. I asked her what the preacher did and she said, "Nothing, he just let it ring." Later, I thought about it and I think he did the right thing. It would have really been embarrassing if he had answered the phone ("Hey, Joe. I'm kind of busy right now, can I call you back? No really, I need to call you back.") or if he'd pulled it out and turned it off. So I'm thinking that if you're ever officiating a wedding and your cell phone rings, just ignore it. Wonder what his ring tone was?

Speaking of churches, I was in another town recently (somewhere near Frost, but without a speed-trap) and drove past a large church that said it was the so-and-so Full Gospel Church. I was thinking, Full Gospel as compared to what? Are there any Half Gospel churches? If so, do they just preach about Matthew and Mark?

Did you know that Larry LaPrise died? He was the person who wrote the song "The Hokey Pokey." He died at a fairly young age and it was very traumatic for his family... especially when they put him in his coffin. They put the right leg in and that's when the trouble started.

A frequently shown Microsoft TV ad shows a cute little 4 1/2 year old little girl uploading photos from her camera to her computer and emailing them to someone else. Four and a half! The only possible reason that Microsoft would run this ad is to irritate me and hundreds of thousands of other techno-challenged older folks. I recently tried to put some photos from my camera into my computer and got a message saying that my monitor (which is brand new) didn't have enough resolution. I need a monitor with more resolve, because I'm running out of it.

Speaking of irritation, do people still burp Tupperware tops? I don't burp them anymore cause I can't ever get them to fit right. The ones I have are a different brand than Tupperware and the tops are slightly smaller than the bowls. I think that Microsoft must have purchased a Tupperware knock-off company and have created just-too-small tops to irritate me. I have begun to hate them. Microsoft and plastic containers.

Did you every think about the fact that there is a word for women haters (misogynist) but no word for man haters? I would guess it's because we guys are so loveable that no one hates us.

I think that beauty shops have the most creative names in the retail world. Just in the Waco phone book you can find: American Hairlines, Nappy Roots, A Cut Above, Anue You, Braids & Fades, Flip Your Wig, Hair We Are, Hairy Situations, Hippie Chic, The Mane Attraction, N 2 Stylz, Sister Scissors, The Snip, The Cutting Edge and The Texas Hair Force. What other business has so much fun with names? A friend in Dallas told me about one there named "Curl Up & Dye".

I recently saw a sign at an establishment that advertised "Semi-Parking". It confused me a little until I realized that it meant parking for 18-wheelers. When I was in college (at The University) I specialized in "semi-parking". I parked on corners, in front of fire hydrants, on yellow lines or wherever the heck I could find a minimum amount of space to put my car. The city of Austin didn't approve of my creative "semi-parking" and put lots of little un-appreciative notices on my windshield. Once, I came home from class and noticed two policemen standing at the front door of my apartment. I went in the back door of my apartment where my roommates told me that the policemen said they had a warrant for my arrest. I thought it over for a minute and decided that they must have the wrong Jack Smith (there are more than one of us) and opened the door to let them in. They said that they had a warrant for my arrest for unpaid parking tickets. Bingo. They had the right Jack Smith. They said all I had to do was go down and pay the fines, but that the city didn't take checks, only cash. I think the total was about $105 but I don't think I'd ever had $105 in cash and my two roommates couldn't pitch in enough to make the total either. So, the two motorcycle policemen led me, in my car, to the campus check-cashing place. One drove in front of me and one behind me. It was my first and last personal motorcycle procession. They then walked into the check-cashing place with me (a local drug store on the Drag) one on my left arm and one on my right arm. I wrote what was probably a hot check, and then we got back in the procession and drove to the police station where I paid my fine and all was forgiven.

I'm sure that parking around the University is even worse today. But I did hear about a creative Austinite who solved the parking problem. He bought a parked car.

Speaking of Austin, I recently had the opportunity to work with a nice lady from Austin who runs a teleprompter service. (And yes, she did get to work her teleprompter for President Obama once in Houston during the campaign, which I imagine is the pinnacle for teleprompter people.) She brings the teleprompter and the computer and runs the thing for people doing TV commercials. I asked her how she got into the teleprompter business. She said that she was looking for a job where she didn't have to wear panty hose. That was the first time I had heard of the "PHJDF" (The Panty Hose Job Determination Factor). Sounds reasonable to me. I wouldn't want a job where I had to wear panty hose either.

While driving around the Waco area, I noticed a church marquee that advertised a "30 Minute Service". Well, why not? In this day of fast food and pay-at-the-pump and drive through banking, why not have fast-church? I think that some religions might encourage occasional fasting, as in abstaining from food, but a 30 minute church "fasting" is a whole new concept. The only problem that I can think of is that you wouldn't have time for much of a nap. I would predict that other churches would get into the competition and one would have a 20 minute service and then another a 15 minute service and then eventually just a drive through, where a recorded voice said "Bless you my son, and please place your offering in the slot at the next window".

I heard a local weatherperson say that our conditions were "extremely mild". I wondered just how mild does something have to be to be "extremely" mild. I mean, that's really, really mild. One of my Father's favorite expressions was "Moderation in all things!" I apparently didn't get his point when it came to parking tickets, but I think he would have also been all for moderation in mildness. You just can't afford to get too extreme in your mildness.

You may have seen the news item about a grackle in San Antonio who hung out in a tree outside of a deli. The grackle, who is apparently not a happy grackle, frequently dive-bombs male customers of the deli as they come and go. No women are attacked, just men, and only men without hats. If this were to spread, it would be a worse pandemic than the swine flu, which we can't call the swine flu cause it makes pigs mad. Mad grackles are enough; we don't want mad pigs to. Instead of dive-bombing, I guess a pig would have to jump-bomb or bump-bomb. Anyway, we don't want it. Mad cows, mad pigs, mad grackles...where will it end? If the grackle dive-bombing trend continues, another tip for you entrepreneurs (did I mention that I love to spell that word?), get in the men's hat business. You're welcome.

Have you ever heard of Deepak Chopra? He's a guy who promotes emotional health through meditation and yoga and all kinds of touchy-feely new-age stuff. I think that Deepak and Oprah should get married because they share a deep level of compassion and understanding of the human condition. Also, it would be great fun for Oprah to be named Oprah Chopra.

WHY DO WE SAY "TUNA FISH" AND NOT SAY "CHICKEN BIRD" OR "STEAK COW?"

Some times when you hear or read the news, you wonder if someone isn't just making it up. One day, a while back, I looked at a local internet news site and there were five items in a row that were incredible, which doesn't mean great, but means not credible, or at least hard to believe.

First was a story about a Bavarian chemist and entrepreneur who is making custom-made contact lenses for animals. They range in size from cat-eye size to fist-width size for rhinos. The first clients have mostly been zoos, but it was said that dozens of house pets, racehorses, circus animals and even guide dogs (you can't have the blind leading the blind) have been customers. The cost was not specifically given other than to say it was "thousands of euros" which is a like a whole bunch more of US dollars. You might be thinking, as I was, that if you can't teach your dog to roll over how in the world would you teach him to put those little contact lenses in their little cases over night. Well, it turns out that the contact lenses are implanted in the animal's eyes with surgery. (How much anesthetic do you have to give a rhino or an elephant? How do you reach a giraffe's eyes?) Anyway, there will soon be a US subsidiary of the Bavarian company in Salt Lake City, so if Spot or Fluffy seem to be having trouble (See Spot Run...into walls) and you have a few extra thousand euros, you can be the first on your block to have a pet with contact lenses.

The second story was a local item about a Gatesville fire truck that was on its way to a fire in the country and came over a hill and ran into two cows, killing them both. The truck was damaged, but fortunately no firemen were injured. I had two questions about this. Did the firemen consider taking the cows with them to the fire and having a barbeque? And secondly, I wondered if the cows had had contact lenses if they would have seen the fire truck coming in time to mosey out of the way.

The third story was also about a wreck. Two people were injured when their car ran off of Valley Mills Drive and into a former Taco Bell building. The restaurant was closed and so was the drive-thru. They should have been able to see that. Maybe they needed a guide dog with contacts that could drive.

The fourth story was about a man in Bryan who placed his head on a railroad track as the train approached. The news said that the police "suspected it was a suicide." Ya think?

The fifth story was about a scientific study that said that smog affects people's IQ. It found, in studying young children, that those who were raised (OK, reared) in smoggy conditions scored lower on IQ tests than those who breathed cleaner air. This is not incredible. It's credible. This could explain Hollywood, Los Angeles and the whole California state government.

Someone told me about a restaurant that served Kobe beef from Japan. Kobe beef comes from some fancy Japanese Wagyu cattle and is supposed to be very good, but very expensive. I looked on the internet and found a web site where you can buy the steaks by mail order and, believe it or not, they were On Sale. You can get two steaks (regularly priced at $190) for almost half price at only $99.99. You do have to cook them yourself and pay for the shipping and handling. I'm not going to order any, but I got to wondering if these fancy cows in Japan have real Japanese cowboys to go with them. If so, I wonder if they like Country-Eastern music?

While watching a football game, I got to thinking about the really great inventions of the last 50 years or so. Right at the top of the list (along with zip-lock bags, the TV remote control and the GPS) is the yellow line that shows on TV where the first down marker is. I don't understand the technology, but it's amazing. The next great invention will be when they figure out how to put that yellow line on the field when you are at the stadium. Seems like some kind of colored laser would work and the referees would never have to measure. It would cause some lost jobs, but hey, who wants to be on a chain gang anyway?

Many of my favorite great inventions involve the automobile. I love air conditioning, power windows and cruise control. The first car I ever owned was a 1951 Chevy. It had no air conditioning, no automatic transmission, no power anything. But instead of air conditioning, there was a rod on the left side of the floorboard that you could pull. The rod would open a little door to the outside and cool air (or hot air) could come in and blow on your feet. Sometimes I wish I still had that option. My feet still miss the breeze. In my first cars, I never had to have an oil change because I changed it gradually by adding a quart every time I filled up with gas (or put in a dollar's worth). A dollar would buy three or four gallons, which would let you go 100 miles or so and in Marlin, that could last for a couple of weeks.

I have a serious recommen-dation to all young people out there, or you can pass it on to a young friend. I wish that I had taken a picture of every car I ever owned and put them in a scrapbook. You should have yourself in the picture beside the car...and then later with your spouse and then your kids or your parents or friends. It would be a great history lesson of your family's growth and of your car history. I bet you would look back at least a couple of times and say, "What was I thinking of when I bought that?" I once owned a Chevy Nova for no apparent reason.

Our postman will probably get a hernia someday bringing us sales catalogs. We get hundreds of them. We got one recently called Whatever Works, that is full of gadgets that I didn't know I needed. One of my favorites is a pair of shoes that makes you lose weight. It is a clog-like shoe that has a built-up toe area. It makes you feel that you are walking up hill...

and therefore you will lose weight. You bet. Well, maybe you'll feel like you're losing weight.

Another gadget is a device that you put in your yard to keep dogs from barking. When a dog barks, the device makes an "ultrasonic" sound that humans can't hear but irritates dogs. My dogs would locate the device and chew it into unrecognizable small pieces within 10 minutes. How do humans know if there really is a sound that they can't hear? How do you know when it breaks? The barking dogs?

Do you remember the famous case that Sherlock Holmes solved because of a dog that didn't bark? What if the perpetrator had an "ultrasonic-anti-dog-barking device"? It wasn't so "elementary" Holmes... it was more like "middle-school."

Also available for dogs there is a collar that is both a pest repellant and has a recorded message that says, "My name is Fido, and I live at 100 Oak Street". I think it's a good idea, but I don't know how you get your dog to talk. My dogs can't talk. They used to bark, but are now afraid I might get an "ultrasonic-anti-dog-barking-device".

We have two new puppies at our house that bite and chew anything within reach. They don't bark much, so their bite is worse than their bark.

There are lots of devices in the catalog to keep things like pools, birdbaths and steps from freezing in the winter. It would be cheaper to just move to Texas.

I like the idea in the catalog of a "nail holder" that keeps you from hammering your fingers and there is designer duct tape, in pretty colors and patterns. How often have you said to yourself, "I wish I had some designer duct tape to wrap this pipe with?" And if you did say that to yourself, why did you end your sentence with a preposition?

Then there's a digital pest repeller. You just plug this little nite-lite looking thingy into a plug and it instantly turns your whole house wiring system into a pest control for mice, rats and roaches. Well, maybe at least the nite-lite would work so the pests could see where they're going.

Then there's the "Goatee Saver/Shaver". It's a piece of plastic shaped like the goatee area of your face that you hold in place with your teeth and it gives you a template to shave around, for accurate goatee shaving. Inaccurate goatee shaving was a problem of which I was not aware.

One last thing was a container into which you put your toothbrush when not in use. It is battery powered with an "Ultraviolet Light Scanner" that kills 99.9% of toothbrush bacteria. I wondered if dogs could hear "Ultraviolet Light"? Oh well, I've never had a dog bark at my toothbrush anyway. If you want to clean your toothbrush, just put it in the dishwasher.

There was an article in the newspaper about a local semi-religious group called the Void Collective. I read the article, but couldn't understand it. I think it would be very difficult to collect voids, although they would be easy to display, I guess. Anywhere you have an empty space you could display more empty spaces. They have a slogan that is "Godisnowhere". That, of course, could be God is Nowhere...or God is Now Here, and I'm more confused. The fact that they meet in a bar doesn't help the confusion. I guess that for communion, you can get wine or mixed drinks.

It will be hard for some young folks to believe, but when I was in school there were no backpacks. We actually had to carry our books in our hands. Can you imagine? I don't know how we survived, especially since we were walking 8 miles to school in the snow and uphill both ways.

I once heard that you have a better chance of getting struck by lightening than winning the lottery. Given the choice, I'll take winning the lottery. But...I also read that in the last dozen years in the USofA 649 people were killed by lightening. That's shocking! 82% of those killed were male. This, of course, isn't fair and there should be a government program to stop the discriminatory actions of lightening. There are more females in the country than males, so they should have the greater share of that once-in-a-lifetime unique lightening experience. The scientist tried to analyze why men were the victims to such a large degree. They looked into whether or not the male cranium had more iron than the female cranium. (Ladies, insert your own "hardheaded" joke here.) They also investigated the conductive properties of testosterone, but couldn't find a link. Their final conclusion was that men are struck more often by lightening because, "they are just kind of stupid."
Well. I either resent or resemble that conclusion. Why should a little lightening stop a fishing or golfing outing? You can't play golf or fish every day. You have to take advantage of the time that you have and your life can't be dominated by the weather.

Speaking of shopping (and surely we were sometime), I see several options in catalogs and stores for heating appliances for your patio or back yard. Chimineas, stone fire pits, tile fire pits. I think I have a better option. When it gets too cold, stay inside. Why would you want to try and heat the cold? What about global warming? The TV's inside anyway.

There have been a lot of people "under the weather" this season, what with all the pandemics. As a matter of fact, 100% of the people have been under the weather. The weather is almost always above us, unless we're on a mountaintop in Colorado or in an airplane. I wonder how that phrase came to be? Well, I looked it up. It was first used by an author, named J. K. Marvel, in 1850 in a book titled "Reveries of a Bachelor". It was used as a synonym for "ill and indisposed" and also for "drunk". That explained who said it, but I'm still not sure why it was said. I would guess that in the old days people gave the weather more credit for illness than they do today, although you will still hear people say that if you get cold and wet, you'll get sick. I think that that's true if your germs or viruses also get cold and wet.

Some friends went to Branson recently and said that among other acts, they saw a really good impersonator who did a lot of 60's and 70's singers like Barry Manilow and Neil Diamond. I wonder if you were going to be a Neil Diamond impersonator you might bill yourself as "Neil Cubic-Zirconium?"

There was a movie called The Perfect Storm. I didn't see it, but it was apparently about a situation wherein all of worst possible weather factors converged to create a really terrible situation. The phrase is now used to define any situation that is unusual and a uniquely bad merger of events. But what, I wonder, would your really perfect storm be? Maybe it would be raining chocolate chip cookies and Blue Bell ice cream?

I've noticed lately that I have trouble taking change from cashiers. Is it just me, or do you have the same problem? Say I'm at the grocery store and buy my groceries and have $3.59 cents in change coming back. The cashier puts the bills flat in his or her hand and then puts the receipt on top of that and then the change on top of that. I have my billfold in one hand and now she tries to hand me this stack of money and receipt. I have to try and get the change off of the stack into my pocket and then put the receipt in a grocery sack, or throw it away, and then put the bills back into my billfold, basically with one hand and I don't do it well. I don't remember what they used to do differently, but it's a crisis that we need to face and overcome.

My favorite new TV show of the season is The Good Wife. It is really well done and Julianna Margulies is very appealing. My second favorite new show is NCIS Los Angeles. It has an actress, Linda Hunt, who plays the boss, "Hetty" Lange. She has been on various TV shows including a stint as a judge on The Practice. She won an Academy Award in 1982 for Best Supporting Actress in the movie The Year of Living Dangerously in which she played a man. She is not short of talent, but is very, very short. Her bio says that she is 4 foot 9 inches, but I would guess she is closer to 4 feet even. I was thinking that if she should ever decide to run for office, she should run in an "At Small" election.

I bought a chair once, but sometimes it seemed more like a footstool than a chair. I couldn't decide which it was. I called the furniture store, and the guy told me it was OK that I was confused, that I had bought an "occasional" chair.

What's the difference in a "footstool" and a "hassock" and an "ottoman"? And don't they all sound archaic? We need a new word. Footpropperupper?

Well, it's March, unless you're really late reading this. If you are, have you been putting off that trip to the Doctor? (I ask this because a lot of people tell me that they read *The Wacoan* while in Doctor's office waiting rooms. Unfortunately, you will probably have time to read the whole magazine...so relax and enjoy.)

One of the bad things about March is that it's time to do your income taxes. Have you ever wondered why they call it a "tax 'return"? It's not like they're going to send your money back. Maybe a better name would be a "tax we-burn". You could put all of your investment money in taxes. They are certain to go up. And remember that real estate taxes may be deductible, but fake estate taxes are not.

The pharmaceutical companies spend a lot of time and money on research to create these expensive, but important drugs. Some PETA types get all upset about testing done on animals. I'm opposed to animal testing also, but for a different reason. I'm afraid they would get a higher score than I would.

You have probably seen civil war reenactments and those WWII air battle reenactments. Well, I was invited to join a group that does Cold War reenactments. It's pretty easy — all we have to do is sit around and look worried about the Soviet Union. The cold war wasn't so hot.

Why do people always say, "May the best man win?" Shouldn't the bridesmaid win sometime?

You probably heard that the post office is losing billions of dollars a month (or is it a day?) and to help solve this problem (is it considered a "problem" when the government loses money?) they might quit delivering mail on Saturdays and raise the price of stamps. I talked to a post office employee and he told me that the Post Office is the only government agency that actually makes money. (This is obviously not counting the mint, which really does actually make money.) He said that the Post Office makes a profit, but that the government takes it away and spends it on other stuff. It's possible. They have been taking Social Security income and using it for other stuff for decades. The problem could also be competition from email and faxes and texting and FedEx and UPS and on-line-bill-paying. But anyway, I don't think not getting mail on Saturday will be a big negative in my life. I can wait until Monday for junk mail and bills.

The post office guy was mad about the "no-mail-on Saturday" deal. I guess it will cut into his overtime, but he wasn't really, really mad as in "going postal." I wonder, if a UPS guy goes off, would it be called "going parcel?"

As I am writing this, the lottery (Power Ball) is huge. I confess to sometimes buying lottery tickets. They say that the lottery is a tax on people who are bad at math. Well, I picked my lottery number from the digital expansion of PI — so there!

A retired banker with years of experience said that when he was a banker, he had to be careful when dealing with the "P" professions. What are the "P" professions, I asked? Plumbers, painters, preachers, politicians and even physicians (apparently they can't do paperwork and sometimes invest in risky schemes.) I guess that printers, pharmacists, postal employees, photographers, physicists and philosophers were OK since he didn't mention them. I don't think I'd loan money to a philosopher. He might decide to rethink his beliefs in that whole banking system concept.

Politicians often borrow money to run a campaign and then lose. Donors don't usually pony-up to losing candidates after the fact, so that's always a risk. When preachers lose their flocks, bankers can lose their socks. Bankers seem to like postal employees, because they are always pushing the envelope. An additional problem for bankers with troubles is that they can't hire policemen, public relations people or private detectives to help. More potential P problems.

I have kind of a P profession. I'm a procrastinator. It's kind-of a profession, because I'm very professional about it. If procrastination were a religion, I'd be the Pope.

Also not on the P list were parents. Parents need strong bank accounts because they will soon discover the expensive nature of children as well as other inconveniences. It might be good if potential parents had to care for a couple of someone else's small children for a while to give them a flavor of what they have in store. It could be thought of it as a "whine tasting."

I had a lingering cough recently. I tried to cough into my elbow like the TV commercials recommend, but sometimes you fail. If a coffer is the person who coughs, is the one on whom he coughs the coffee?

The revolution may be coming because the Nanny State is planning to reduce the amount of salt in our food. This is raising my blood pressure more than salt does. There is no salt substitute. Some of us humans have an innate taste for salt, which is needed for some healthy, basic biological functions, I'm sure. Salt is used as a preservative to inhibit microbial growth; it gives texture and structure to certain foods and most importantly…it tastes good. Soon, salt users will be treated like smokers. We'll have to go outside to salt our food. In the words of Charlton Heston, they will have to pry my saltshaker from my cold, dead hand.

More nanny state news. County officials in Santa Clara County in California (San Jose area) have voted to ban restaurants from giving away toys with meals. They want to take the "happy" out of Happy Meals in order to protect their little darlings from high-calorie meals aimed at kids. Thank goodness. How does a county government decide it can tell McDonald's what to sell?

Here's a quick quiz. What do the following words have in common? Koa, Vlad, Alterraun, Akwasi, Crezdon, Fendi, Deji, Jorrick, Selvish, Sherrick, Syd'quan and Ndamukong. These are the first names of soon-to-be-very-rich-young-men who were drafted last month by NFL teams. Wasn't a Jack Smith in the bunch. It's a pity. I could have been a contender.

What is a better feeling than coming over a hill and seeing a policeperson with radar looking at you as you drive by while going slightly below the speed limit without having to hit your breaks? Ha Ha. Didn't get me. You can get a rush by not rushing.

Thinking "outside the box" is good, unless, of course, it's your cat doing the thinking.

There are a lot of golf tournaments for charities this time of year. A friend asked me if I wanted to play in one and I told him it was too hot. He said I should reconsider because it was for handicapped kids. I thought, "Hey, I might have a chance to win that one."

I decided that I needed to be more organized so I bought a Day Planner. Unfortunately, all of the pages were blank. I have no idea what I'm supposed to do tomorrow.

I WONDER WHY WAITPERSONS ARE SUPPOSED TO GET 15% AND CHURCHES 10%. BETTER UNION?

I was driving down 18th street and saw a retail store with a large sign outside that said, "HUGE DRESS SALE." So, if you're looking for a huge dress... that's the place to go.

In the same week in November, I went to a wedding and a funeral. At both events, the first song played was a song that was new to me, called *I Can Only Imagine*. It's a contemporary Christian song and it's very nice and many of you will be familiar with it. I don't have any real relationship with contemporary Christian music...my church is so old fashioned, we sing hymns. But, anyway, I was surprised that the same song worked for a funeral and a wedding. I looked it up and it has been recorded by dozens of groups and individuals, but the originator is a group called MercyMe. As I interpret the words, it talks of imaging how things will be after death in heaven. This, of course, is natural for a funeral. But for a wedding... are we thinking of being in wedded bliss as in heaven or we thinking of the end of our life, as in death. Guess it depends on the spouse.

We should all stay married, because as they say... love is grand. Divorce is a hundred grand.

For a new year's resolution this year, I vowed to procrastinate more. But now I think I'll probably wait until next year. I also resolved to finish whatever I sta

When FDR said, "All we have to fear is fear itself," do you think he just forgot about snakes & spiders?

Have you noticed that whenever a TV interviewer concludes an interview and says, "Thank you, Mr. Jones," that Mr. Jones always says "Thank you?" The appropriate response to "thank you" is "you're welcome" but they almost never say it. They say "thank you." I think it's because they really are thankful that they got their 15 minutes of fame on TV.

I have a friend who said she thought her 10-year-old son was going to be a dentist. She said she was pretty sure of it, because he was already saving old magazines.

Speaking of doctors, we all know that "An apple a day keeps the doctor away." I wonder what kind of fruit would keep the lawyer away?

I couldn't make this up. It was reported that the folks in Saudi Arabia had captured and detained a vulture from Israel. We're talking about a real bird. A large bird with an 8-foot wingspan. The bird was accused of being an Israeli spy because the Saudi's found a GPS transmitter on the bird. The Israelis said it was a common tracking device used to keep up with the vulture's whereabouts because vultures are an endangered species. I don't know what happened to the accused bird, but under normal Saudi justice he or she was probably executed. Then we get the story about the 3,000 black birds that committed suicide in Arkansas. No one seems to know why. I think the Arkansas birds had a mass suicide to protest the arrest and treatment of their feathered friend in Saudi Arabia. How did the Arkansas birds hear about the incident in Saudi Arabia? A little birdie told them.

The Super Bowl was pretty good this year. But the game may have gotten less attention than the commercials, the half time show and the singing of the National Anthem. The commercials seemed less interesting than usual, although I did like the VW spot with the kid dressed like Darth Vader and the Chevy truck ad for the little boy who got stuck in the well, caught in a cave, swallowed by a whale and involved with a volcano. Would a bowl of black-eyed peas have been as entertaining as the group The Black Eyed Peas at the half time show? I know. I'm too old.

The National Anthem is a difficult song to sing. Both the words and the music are difficult. It takes a talented singer to do it well. Why in the world do sporting events get rock stars to try to sing it? They trick it up so badly that it's terrible, even when they can remember the words. How about the Army or Navy or Air Force choir? How about the Mormon Tabernacle Choir? Many years ago I was part of a barbershop quartet in Marlin. We were known as the Marlin Fishing Tackle Choir. We could have done a better job than Christina Aguilera.

I know you have witnessed the protests in the streets of Egypt and other places around the world. The protestors always throw rocks at tanks and policemen. The efficacy of throwing a rock at a tank is another matter, but my first question is where do they get the rocks? If I were to start a protest in Downtown Waco, I don't think I could find a single rock. Maybe there's a new business opportunity for you entrepreneurs. Rock provider. Want to protest? Call 1-800 Rock Stock. We show, you throw.

A scientist/biology professor at the University of Colorado says that plants can be created that will be able to detect bombs. She says that plants have receptors in their dermal tissue (I think that would be the leaf) and that they can be made to respond to certain pathogens floating in the air. It would be many years away, because now it takes several hours or days for the plant to give a noticeable reaction, like turning from green to white. Finding out about a bomb several hours or days later isn't too swift, even for a government agency and I'll bet we soon hear from the bomb-sniffing-dog's union. You know how an undercover spy is called a "plant"? Well someday when you go to the airport you won't know if the ficus is a plant, or just a plant.

I was throwing away some old phone books recently and it occurred to me that old telephone books would make ideal personal address books. Just cross out the names and addresses of people you don't know.

Can't find your way to the smart-phone store? There's a map for that!

They say that a tomato is a fruit, although it seems more like a vegetable to me. If a tomato really is a fruit, does that make ketchup a smoothie? And how many ways are there to spell ketchup. "Catchup" and "catsup" have both been used through the years. I looked it up. "Ketchup" was first used way back in 1711, "catsup" in 1730 and "catchup" in 1690. I think I'll go with "catchup". I can spell it without having to think.

Speaking of food, if I ever start a new restaurant that sells only very healthy donuts, I think I'll call it "Hole Foods Market".

Sometimes we are told to use a "back-slash" in a computer address. Not a forward slash, but a back-slash. Fortunately, my computer keyboard has only one slash that I can find. I don't know if it's a back or forward slash. How do you tell? Is the top pointing forward, or the bottom pointing backward? Anyway, just use the slash (/) on the same key as the ? and it will all work out.

Sometimes my satellite TV reception is interrupted by rain. Once I was trying to watch 20/20. The reception was so spotty that it was like I was trying to watch 20/40.

I've noticed lately when looking at new car ads that the top end of the car model is frequently called the "Limited". If that car is the "top of the line", why not call it the "Unlimited"? What's limited about it? Maybe the price "limits" the number of buyers?

There was a news item recently that quoted a study saying that frequent church attendees were more overweight than non-attendees. If that's true, I wonder why? I almost never see anybody eating during church. Communion food isn't fattening. Maybe it's the eating after church. My mother used to fry chicken on most Sundays and there would be mashed potatoes and gravy and rolls and butter and lots of fattening stuff. But when was the last time people cut up and fried a chicken at home? The fifty's? I wouldn't begin to know how to neatly cut up a chicken. I can, however, do a great job of ordering a Bush's #1 with fries and a coke.

Speaking of church, a friend said that with the popularity of biblical names these days, he is kind of surprised at the reaction he gets when people meet his grandson, Satan.

Do you feel tired and run-down in the middle of the afternoon, especially after a large lunch? There's a nap for that.

Now that spring is here, I'd like to establish a no-fly zone around my back porch and gas grill.

You see a lot of ads on TV and hear some on radio encouraging you to buy gold. Some say that it's a good idea to invest in precious metals. I looked into it, but they're way too expensive for me. So now I'm looking around trying to get a good deal on some metals that are just kinda cute.

DID YOU EVER WONDER WHY RIGHT-HANDED BASEBALL PITCHERS AREN'T CALLED NORTHPAWS? ME NEITHER.

I met a fellow recently who said that he read my column frequently. I thanked him and then he said, "Each of your columns is better than the next." I'm pretty sure that that was not a good thing.

It's the story of my life. A redheaded stepchild rode right past me on a rented mule, and there I was without a whip.

A friend said that his aunts used to come up to him at family weddings, poke him in the ribs, cackle and tell him, "You're next." He said they stopped doing that after he started doing the same thing to them at funerals.

If I were ever to master the metric system, it would be a major kilometerstone.

There has been a lot of haggling in the Texas legislature this year concerning education funding. At my recent high school reunion we reminisced about our school days in Marlin High School. The Superintendent had an office on the second floor of the high school building and he had a secretary (administrative assistants hadn't been invented yet) who was also the school district's bookkeeper. The high school principle had an office a couple of doors down and he had a secretary. The junior high principle was on the first floor and he didn't have an office. He worked out of his history classroom and had no assistant. The elementary principal (for awhile it was my Grandmother) had one secretary. That was a grand total of seven people in administration for the entire school district. We got a great education. Today in major school districts there may be 7 people in the high school curriculum department. Times have certainly changed. For the better?

It was distressing recently to hear about and see news video of the wildfires near Possum Kingdom Lake. But it made me think. Why would you name a place or a lake "Possum Kingdom"? I have had some recent experience with a possum coming into my garage in the dark of night and eating my dog's and cat's food and tearing stuff up. They are basically disgusting animals if they are in your yard and you surely don't want them to create a kingdom. How many possums are in a kingdom? Would you name a recreational lake after a large rat?

Speaking of news, the homeland security folks have warned that terrorists and some of their doctors might develop a way to put bombs inside the human body, which would be very difficult to spot when going through airport security. One thing mentioned was bombs put in breast implants. Wow. Talk about a booby-trap.

I was at a meeting recently where there was a straw poll. Attendees were given little plastic drinking straws as they arrived and encouraged to "vote" by dropping their straw in a selection of sacks that were marked with political candidates names. It was a cute idea. One of the attendees mentioned to me that it wasn't really a "straw" poll...but a "plastic" poll. He was right. Picky, but right. I then begin to wonder why the drinking instrument that is made of paper or plastic...is called a "straw". I guess that there was once a kind of straw that one could drink through? If so, what did the liquid taste like? Straw? And then why do we have black berries, blue berries and "straw" berries. Where is the straw? Maybe someone stole it to drink out of. (Yes, kids...a preposition is something you should never end a sentence with.)

Somebody came up with the fifty coolest names in college football history. They are real names, not nicknames. Among them were: Yourhighness Morgan, Immaculate Perfection Harris, Taz Knockum, Lawyer Tillman and Lawyer Milloy, Mister Simpson, Golden Tate, Brit Barefoot, Knowledge Timmons, Ray Ray McElrathbay, Major Applewhite, Prince Amakmara, Hurcules Satele, Co-Eric Riley, LeQuantum McDonald (Baylor's entry, apparently he's into physics), D'Brickashaw Ferguson, Preacher Pilot, Pistol Pete Pedro, Colt McCoy and Sonny Sixkiller. I wonder if Co-Eric had a twin brother?

There was a news item recently about someone thinking that it might be a good idea to remove obese children from their homes, indicating that this might be a form of parental abuse. This would make a great government jobs program. The US of A Government could hire about a million folks to go door to door and weigh children. They could carry a chart with them indicating the proper weight, based on age or size or some combination, and if the kid is too heavy, just grab him or her and off they go to the regional fat-kid farm, where the kids would daily feast on celery and lettuce (or arugula) and other "Unhappy Meals". Parents could achieve visitation rights if they joined Weight Watchers or The Biggest Loser. Deciding whether to remove a child from his home based on weight would give new meaning to the "Scales of Justice".

You may have heard that there is a financial problem with our government. Seems like there was a recent controversy about a ceiling for debt. Well, we proved we could break through that sucker. There was a front-page headline in a national newspaper that said, "Families Slice Debt to Lowest is 6 Years". There seems to be a big difference in spending when you're spending your own money versus politicians spending "government" money. Oh well, when those formerly unemployed one million fat-kid-weighers start sending their income taxes to Washington, we should be OK.

A friend emailed that he might just get one of those "eye phones." If he really turns high-tech, he could get an ear phone with his eye phone. I wonder if sailors have "aye-aye-phones"?

Sometimes I think we should rename "software" to "softwhere." As in, where the heck do I click to fix this?

I got a message from my car's computer that said I should check the coolant level. I did and it looked like it could use a little, so I went to the store. They still call it anti-freeze and/or anti-freeze/coolant. I remember as a young driver that we were always told to make sure that we had enough anti-freeze in the winter. Why did we do that in Texas? Did you ever hear of a Texas car freezing? I didn't.

Speaking of cars, I see some really ugly cars on the road and on new car lots. Cars, for instance, that look like square boxes with wheels. Some people obviously like them or they wouldn't still be around. I would be hard pressed to come up with an advertising campaign for these ugly cars, but the best I could come up with is, "Kiss your car theft fears goodbye!"

I understand that God didn't create anything without a purpose, but I'm a little confused about mosquitoes and roaches. And speaking of mosquitoes, the terrible summer heat led to very few mosquitoes. I don't think I saw (or felt) one in June, July or August. Do you think they are gone forever? I didn't see many flies either. I guess it was too hot to fly.

A guy on the radio said that due to the extreme heat that a lot of flowers that normally were present, weren't around this year and that we should put up humming bird feeders because the little birds were having a hard time finding nectar. So...I bought a humming bird feeder and filled it with sugar water and hung it up. It took about 30 minutes for the humming birds to find it and either lots of them have, or a couple of them have a serious drinking problem. Do you know why they're called "humming" birds? They can't remember the words.

I get tired of the three-letter acronyms use in texting, like LOL and OMG. It seems like almost everything is identified by a stupid three-letter acronym, or TLA's, as I call them.

I wonder if there's one of those familiar books about ventriloquism? One called "Ventriloquism for Dummies?"

Did you hear about the Siamese twins who moved to England, so the other one could drive? I didn't either.

There has been a lot of talk lately about the high cost of a college education. Students and parents end up with huge student loan debts that take years to pay off, and the costs keep on rising. I think I may have a solution. Home schooling for college students. Sure, it would take more time and study for the Mom/Teachers out there, but the Dads could help with PE and intramurals and the beer parties. Not sure what we'd do about a football team.

Last month was the 70th anniversary of Pearl Harbor and the start of our country's involvement in WWII. Folks at the time, and later, said they would never buy products from our former enemies. Today I'm driving a German car and watching a Japanese television. I wonder if in another 70 years, we'll be driving Al-Qaeda cars and watching Taliban televisions?

Hope you had a Happy Groundhog Day. It's a holiday (kinda sorta) that no one can really object to except maybe the groundhog that gets pulled out of his groundhog hole. There are several things about Groundhog Day that are weird, the first being...why does it exist? I looked it up and it started as a Pennsylvania German celebration over 160 years ago, but I don't really know why. The groundhog (or hedge hog), which is a rodent, comes out of his hole (with help from a human puller) and looks around. If he sees his shadow, he figures that there will be six more weeks of winter, so he goes back in his hole. If he (or she...it could be Punxsutwaney Phyllis) doesn't see his or her shadow, it means that spring is just around the corner, so he or she can stay out of the hole. This is counter-intuitive. If the sun is shining that should mean that spring is nearer than if it's cloudy and cold...but what do you expect from a large rodent? How accurate is the annual prediction? Groundhog Day proponents say that it is accurate 75 to 95 percent of the time. Actual scientific studies say that is accurate only 39% of the time. Therefore the groundhog has about the same degree of accuracy as real meteorologists.

I usually don't watch the Grammy awards, because they don't relate much to me or my musical tastes, but this year I watched...probably because of the interest in how they would handle the Whitney Houston death. It turns out that more people watched than ever before, probably for the same reason. I thought they handled the Whitney issue with respect and the proper amount of attention. They didn't overdo it. The show was entertaining. I was not familiar with Adele, but learned about her on the 60 Minutes program prior to the Emmy's. She is very unique in today's entertainment world. She doesn't wear costumes, dance or find her self surrounded by weird male dancers. She just stands at the microphone and sings. Beautifully. Good for her. She had a polyp on her vocal cords and had to quit singing for several months and wasn't allowed to talk for two months. I can't imagine any female that I know not being able to speak for two months. (Well, I can imagine it.) Adele won six Grammy's including Best Record and Best Song. I don't know what the difference is.

Admiral Hyman Rickover once said that "Great minds discuss ideas, average minds discuss events and small minds discuss people." So...I want to talk about people at the Grammy's.

I had not heard of Bruno Mars. His act was great. The band was all dressed alike in shiny gold sports coats just like the doo-wop bands of the 50's. They danced like the doo-wop bands and did a James Brown dance impersonation. It was great. On the other hand, Cold Play was very cold. Little Stevie Wonder isn't, but Taylor Swift is (little or swift). The Foo Fighters made you go look in the refrigerator or organize your sock drawer, and there was an electronic music interlude that was more stressful than going to the dentist. Someone named Nicki Minaj has serious mental issues, and Chris Brown is better at assaulting girl friends than singing. He should get a day job. I think that the excessive number of male dancers were used in hopes of covering up some bad, repetitious music. It didn't work. So much for the rantings of an old dude.

Oh, well. Mark Twain once said, "Richard Wagner's music is better than it sounds." Maybe that's true of some of today's music.

Speaking of old dudes, the Grammy's had Glen Campbell, Paul McCartney, the Beach Boys and Tony Bennett. That's a combined age of about 550. Glen has Alzheimer's, but can still remember the unusual words to "Rhinestone Cowboy". "With a subway token and a dollar tucked inside my shoe...There'll be a load of compromisin...on the way to my horizon"

Still speaking of old dudes, Vicki said that when she first met me she knew that I was "Mr. Right." She just didn't know that my first name was "Never."

I read the obituaries every day to see who's left the playing field. I recently read that Cautious Thompson had died. I guess she just wasn't cautious enough.

I recently read that England had a contest for the joke of the year. This was the winner: "I had a car crash the other day. A dwarf got out of the other car and said, I'm not happy. To which I replied, Which one are you then?"

I liked the one that came in third place better. It was: "Conjunctivitis.com – that's a site for sore eyes.

Since I moved my office to my home, I've become more involved in cooking and even in some grocery shopping. Have you noticed that you can get "home-style cooking" in restaurants and "restaurant-style" food in grocery stores? It seems we always want to be where we aren't.

Some place we usually don't want to be is at the doctor's office, except for the excellent opportunity it gives us to read *The Wacoan* in the waiting room. Sometimes I wonder about my doctor. He recently recommended that I have an MRI to determine whether or not I'm claustrophobic.

Has anyone ever paid full price at Joseph A. Banks?

You may have heard about a man in New York who attempted to rob a bank using a plunger as his weapon of choice. Maybe he was an unemployed plumber or maybe he really was the dimmest bulb in the chandelier. Maybe he had heard about the bad-old-days when gangs used to pillage and plunder...and was confused and thought he was supposed to pillage and plunger. He should have gone to the drive-thru and tried to plunge the plastic money tube. Oh well, maybe they will allow him a plunger in his cell. But not a cell phone.

Did you see that in New Jersey you can be fined $250 to $1,000 dollars for having a dog or cat in your car without a seat belt on? Really? What about gerbils? What about gold fish? There are now harnesses for pets that can be snapped into a seat belt apparatus. Can you get your cat into a harness? You can put the animal in a carrier, but it has to be buckled down also. What's the difference in the $250 fine and the $1,000 fine? Size of the dog. Size of the cat scratch? Size of the state's budget deficit? How can you put your dog in a seat belt and still let him hang his head out of the window? One more reason for living in Texas.

I read a report from a writer who went to a college graduation and was surprised to see folks in cutoffs, sleeveless T-shirts, shorts, ball caps and one in a bathing suit. (None that he could see had hair rollers.) It shouldn't have been a surprise. Inappropriate dress, like inappropriate language, is now appropriate in the eyes of many folks. I can remember when folks used to dress up to go to the grocery store. There should be a happy medium somewhere. The concept of "No shirt...No shoes...No problem" should be replaced with common sense. I recently saw a man at a funeral wearing coveralls. Well, at least they were clean. Yeah, I know. If the music is too loud, you're too old.

Speaking of age, Beau Hossler, a 17-year-old high school junior and great golfer, at one point was the leader at the US Open this year. He is baby faced and has braces on his teeth and had his Dad caddying for him. It was great while it lasted. He ended up eight strokes behind the leader and came in second place for top amateur. Frequently, when a golfer wins a PGA event and leaves the 18th hole, he is approached by a gorgeous young blond, his wife or girl friend. Beau was also approached and hugged by a beautiful, young blonde. It was his Mom.

I was filling out forms in a doctor's office. It asked whom they should call in case of an emergency. That's easy. They should call 911. I thought everybody knew that.

There has been a lot of news about the Higgs boson. It has something to do with the origin of matter (as if it matters) and scientists are beside themselves. That's because no one else wants to be beside them, if they get that excited about a boson. I had never heard of Mr. Higgs or a "boson." I looked it up. Though just one letter off, a boson is much different than a bosom. The dictionary says that a boson is "a particle whose spin is zero." That's kind of what I thought. You just can't trust a spinning particle. I can see more taxpayer funded government grants in the offing.

I recently found myself in a fancy store aimed at extracting money from fancy women. (OK, it was Neiman's) If you wonder why I was there...I was a hostage. But while there, I saw a new product that apparently thinks it could rid a fancy lady of cellulite. The product was called Fat Girl Soap. Now who is going to grab a box of Fat Girl Soap and head to the checkout counter? "Hi, I'd like to buy this for a friend."

Also while in Neiman Marcus (also known as Needless Markup) I looked at men's neckties. They were pretty nice. They were $195 each. Who's going to take one of those to the checkout counter? "Hi, I'm buying this for an idiot. Me."

Did you enjoy the Olympics? Did you see the synchronized swimming and the synchronized diving? It makes whatever you're doing a whole lot harder if you have to do it in the same way and at the same time as another person. If they really want tough competition, why stop at swimming and diving? How about synchronized high jumping or synchronized pole vaulting? Synchronized beach volleyball? I'd like to see synchronized table tennis (we call it ping pong in Falls County). The serve would be fairly easy, but the return would be heck.

A good name for a retail establishment lets you know what they do. A group of us were in Salt Lake City a while back and drove past a motel with a great name. It was the Sleep Cheap Motel. That pretty much says it all. I recommend SLC. It's a very clean and historically interesting place. The folks there are very friendly. Kind of like Texas.

For Father's Day a friend of mine got a coffee mug that said "World's Best Dad." Maybe I'm just a sore loser, but it seems to me that there was some nepotism involved in that award.

A while back, there was a Miss Central Texas beauty pageant. The day before, Miss Texas, who was supposed to be a judge, called and backed out. I was called and asked if I could be a replacement judge. It's kind of like being a replacement referee in the NFL. You're not expected to do a good job, but somebody has to do it. Since I have a very boring life and had no plans for Saturday night, I said "Sure." It was a very pleasant afternoon and evening and there were many well qualified candidates. One of the other judges (not a replacement) was a semi-professional judge from the Dallas area. He does this a lot. He had recently been a judge at the Miss Kansas Pageant. He said that the pageant organizers wanted the young ladies there to be able to answer tough questions about the contentious issues of the day, including the topic of abortion. The semi-pro judge didn't want to just ask, "What do you think about abortion?"...so he instead asked, in individual interviews, "When do you think life begins?" He asked the first five girls that question and got the following answers. Three said, "When you get to college." One said, "When you get to high school." And one said, "When you get your driver's license." I think the driver's license answer was correct but I don't know that much about abortion.

One of the girls in the Miss Kansas pageant got her good looks from her father. He's a plastic surgeon.

A lady sat on a black marble bench outside of Cowboy stadium last summer when the temperature was 101. She burned her buttocks. She has now sued the Cowboys and Jerry Jones for her injuries. She claims that Jerry should have, but didn't, warn her that she shouldn't sit on hot black things when it is 101. She was burned and mad. It's a perfect example of hot cross buns. I think Jerry should have warned her about getting involved with ambulance chasing lawyers. He also should have warned her to look both ways before crossing a street and not to run with scissors in her hands. I'm not against suing Jerry Jones. But sue him for being a lousy football team general manager. He didn't warn us about that either.

Someone said something recently about the fall of the Ottoman Empire. I don't know anything about that. I don't know what made it fall or where it fell from or when it fell...but it made me think about places named after furniture. Probably the coolest place named after furniture lately is Davenport, Iowa.

My Dad had an expression to indicate that someone didn't know what he was talking about. He would say, as an example, that so-and-so knows as much about such-and-such as "a pig knows about Sundays". While pigs don't know anything about Sundays, I think my dog does. He's a little down on Sundays because there's no postman to bark at. (Postman is, of course, an archaic word. It should be "Male Postperson.")

This is a true story. A friend recently had surgery that lasted for seven hours. After about four hours the surgeon came out to talk to the family. Instead of immediately going back into surgery he headed out to his car, "to have a cigarette and a Diet Dr Pepper." What's the world coming to when a Doctor can't smoke in the operating room?

I was recently in a large grocery store parking lot and saw a young man pushing about 20 shopping carts at once. The kid was really selfish. Didn't he realize that other people need carts too?

CHAPTER FOUR

Food

My random thoughts seem to frequently be related to eating.
Never write a column on an empty stomach. Use paper or a computer.

Still speaking of food, and we were, I wonder why deviled eggs are
called deviled eggs. What in the devil did they do to deserve that name?
Webster says that one definition of "devil" is to "highly season." Sometimes
I think that Webster may have been hitting the sauce, and not the seasoning
sauce. But maybe, if you put too much pepper and "wooster sauce" in the
hard-boiled egg yoke, it becomes as hot as the devil. Maybe not.

Is it just me, or does anyone else resent flavored potato chips?
It adds unnecessary time to grocery shopping. You have to be extremely
observant or you'll get home with brussels sprout-flavored chips. If I
want a potato chip that tastes like ranch dressing, I can dip one in ranch
dressing. I accidentally had a jalapeno potato chip once that should have
been called a deviled potato chip.

Some folks would be shocked to learn that I'm a natural food
aficionado. Well, at least a few natural foods. Well, mostly one natural food.
I love salt. What could be more natural than salt? It comes right out of the

ground. It's like the "salt of the earth," and that's a good thing. It's the most natural food. It has no preservatives. It is a preservative. I put salt on most everything. Meat, fruit, vegetables. My wife complains when I salt Fritos, but I only do it when they need it and they don't need more

salt as often as potato chips do. I tried to instill in my children the first rule of eating. "Salt before you taste." If you have trouble taking your blood pressure medicine, do like I do...add salt. And if you're having trouble taking your cholesterol medicine, wrap the pills in bacon. It works for me.

I don't think they would like my kind in a Whole Foods Market. I went to one in Austin one time and tried to buy some chicken wings, but they said I had to buy the Whole chicken. I didn't even ask about a steak.

I have a friend on the Atkins Diet. The Atkins diet is like disco music. It comes back every few years for no apparent reason. Anyway, my friend is eating lots of meat and cheese and has lost some weight. I don't have a serious weight problem (he said, hoping to hear the nod of a head in agreement), but most of us can stand to lose a few pounds. So I was thinking of kind of a modified Atkins Diet. Maybe the Half-Atkins Diet. I don't really want to change my current dietary habits too much, but I could easily increase my intake of meat and cheese. So what I was thinking was, that if I left everything else alone, but instead of eating regular hamburgers, I had double-meat, double-cheese hamburgers, I could lose quite a few pounds.

I ate lunch recently at my favorite Austin restaurant, Hoffbrau Steaks, established in 1934 (August 4th to be specific), which hasn't changed a chair or table or even dusted since that day. A guy at the next table asked for a doggie bag. That seemed kind of out-dated. Today we usually ask for "to-go-containers" or "take-out-boxes." We no longer pretend it's for our dog, we just want a free meal later. In the old days, did people really take food to the dog, or were they lying? My wife frequently takes "to-go" food home where it stays in the refrigerator for several days before it's thrown away.

Is "fasting" called "fasting" cause it's the "fastest" way to lose weight? If so, should "self-discipline" be called "slowing?" Just wondering.

I heard on the radio that the cost of bottled water was 900 times that of tap water. Tap water is certified to be OK by the government. You don't know where bottled water comes from. It is only certified to be expensive.

Well, at least you get a cute little squeeze bottle. One that you can refill with tap water at 900 times less cost.

I met a nice lady in the generic section of the grocery store. Her name was "Woman."

DOES THE PHRASE "BATTERED WOMEN" HAVE A WHOLE DIFFERENT MEANING TO A CANNIBAL?

I heard an ad on the radio for diet dog food. Has it come to this? The government says that 66% of us are overweight or obese and we're worrying about fat dogs. Don't buy diet dog food; just give them the lean table scraps, like lettuce or celery. (If I tried to give my dog lettuce, he would bite the hand that fed him.)

There is a current TV commercial for Long John Silvers that advertises a "Go Fish Snack Sandwich". Every time I hear it, I think they say a "Gold Fish Snack Sandwich" and I don't want one. How big could it be?

I think that Italian food is probably better in the US than in Italy. Because we use imported cheese and they only use domestic.

Speaking of eating, I kind of think you have bad eating habits if you use a grocery cart in a convenience store. In other "cooking/eating" news, I found that a hard-boiled egg is hard to beat.

I heard about a couple that got married at the State Fair of Texas in October. Their wedding cake was fried and on a stick.

If you were shopping in a grocery store and saw a can of worms... do you think it would have a "Do Not Open" warning label on it?

One of the dumbest ideas that man (that's a genetic term for humankind) has ever had was the production of ethanol. It probably was a man, the non-generic kind. Ethanol is not only totally worthless as a fuel; it is costing each of us a fortune in increased food prices. Only congress could try to do something good and have it turn out so badly. We generally don't get too concerned about things that affect the economy, unless it affects us directly. Well, now I've been affected. The increased price of corn has increased the price of Fritos and that's where I draw a line in the sand, or a line in the line at the grocery store. It's past time to stop the madness. Outlaw ethanol or there may be a return of the Frito Bandito.

Speaking of food, I see a Wendy's commercial that advertises "one-handed" fast food. That's for those of you who are so busy that you have to eat with one hand and do some work with the other. Has it come to this? About the only multi-tasking that I can do while eating is watching TV and a lot of TV shows will make you lose your appetite.

Speaking of food, I'm not on the selection committee or anything, but I can almost guarantee a Nobel Prize for anyone who can make liver or collard greens taste like bacon.

Did you see the article from the Times of India about a scientific study done at Oxford University? What? You don't read the Times of India? You don't follow scientific studies from Oxford? Well, that's what the internet is for....to bring you weird information that you would never see otherwise. Anyway, this study showed that if you are a vegetarian you might want to reconsider your diet. It says "Eating Veggies Shrinks the Brain." It did not say that vegetarians were brainless, just that they were susceptible to "brain shrinkage."

This study has confirmed what I've suspected for a long time. People who don't like steak or hamburgers or ham or turkey or chicken or bacon or Uncle Dan's barbeque have a screw loose, or at least a shrinking screw. The study says that the brain shrinkage has to do with the lack of vitamin B12, which comes from meat, particularly liver, milk and fish. Forget the liver and maybe the milk. Just eat more meat and fish. I didn't know it before, but B12 is my favorite vitamin.

The study also showed that heavy drinkers had more brain shrinkage than non-drinkers. Well, duh. Most at risk were women in their seventies. How many heavy drinking women in their seventies do you know? "Put the booze down Granny, your brain is shrinking!" The study also said that beer is not as bad as wine for brain shrinkage. So, I figure if Joe Sixpack will eat a sufficient amount of barbeque with his beer, it will all balance out.

Speaking of food and eating out, we all face a major problem in Mexican restaurants. I don't think that Oxford University has done a study about this crisis, but they should. When you salt the chips in the basket, the salt doesn't stay on the chips. It falls to the bottom of the basket. This is mostly because the chips are in a perpendicular position and the law of gravity applies even in Mexican restaurants. They could take the chips and lay them out in horizontal layers so that the salt would stay where it is intended, but the chips are frequently curly so that still wouldn't work well, and you would have to re-salt after you've eaten each layer. I'm not really sure how to cure this problem. I've been known to salt the chips individually, but that is a lot of trouble & sometimes people look at me strangely.

I'm even a little peeved at the Girl Scouts. I ate three boxes of "Thin Mints" & didn't lose a pound.

One food product that I enjoy is "I Can't Believe It's Not Butter." The taste is kind of... unbelievable. I mixed some real butter with some I Can't Believe It's Not Butter, and I can partly believe in it, but not totally.

Because of Christmas shopping, I have spent more time in parking lots lately than is normal for me. Is it just me, or is it everybody? I drive a small to medium sized sedan. 95% of the time, when I'm ready to back out of a parking place, there will be a very large truck or SUV parked to my right that I can't see around, to safely back out. It's usually a black truck or SUV. I creep out and really can't see until I'm way out in the drive area and about half the time someone will honk at me, so I drive back in, wait, and start over again. I think it's a conspiracy. Black helicopters, black pickups, black SUV's. It's a government thing. But why are they after me?

As you know, it's hard to compete with nature for food. When God made the tomato or potato or avocado...it's almost impossible to beat. But occasionally man comes close. I'm thinking of Reese's peanut butter cups. I think Mr. Reese should have won the Nobel Peace Prize for artfully combining chocolate and peanut butter. I recently bought a new-to-me product called Reese's Minis (unwrapped mini cups). They are heavenly. I was a little confused by the package, however, which said the minis were King Size. I guess it's like jumbo shrimp.

I frequently have Coke and Reese's for breakfast. I highly recommend it. The Breakfast of Champions. There are several things that I can eat for a meal that you might not have tried. I can make a meal of Fritos and olives. I can make a meal of saltine crackers and I Can't Believe It's Not Butter. Healthy eating is overrated.

Speaking of health and food... a friend said he'd been to the gym and that they had a great new machine. But he said he could only use it for half an hour before he started to feel sick. He said it had KitKats, Mars Bars, Snickers, Potato Chips...everything he needed.

Still speaking of food, I bought a box of animal crackers and it said on it "Do not eat if seal is broken." So I opened up the box, and sure enough...

And still speaking of food, why do restaurants serve salads with pieces of lettuce about the size of a post card? You can't possibly put it all in your mouth and it's very awkward to cut the lettuce into smaller pieces while in the salad bowl. Why don't they cut it for us? Could it be another government conspiracy? Are there black olives involved?

Mary had a little lamb. Her husband had a little veal. Which reminds me of a true story from my college days. We frequented a restaurant on The Drag in Austin. Sometimes I would order the chicken fried stead and sometimes a veal cutlet. I couldn't really tell the difference so I once asked the waiter what the difference was. He said that they put the gravy on top of the chicken fried steak and on the bottom of the veal cutlet. I think he was telling the truth.

Another favorite Austin spot, the San Jacinto Mexican food restaurant, had a terrifically funny waiter named Raymond or Ramon depending on his ethnic mood of the day. Raymond had a series of gags that he would perform whenever we had someone new at our table. For instance, the new guy would order the Regular Mexican Dinner. When Ramon served the new guy, as he put the plate down, he would say "Liver and Onions". The new guy would invariably complain that that wasn't what he ordered, before looking down at his Regular Mexican Dinner. If the meal delivery ever seemed slow, Raymond would come by the table and say, "Sorry it's taking so long. The cook went out to eat."

I THINK THAT SLIM JIMS ARE PRETTY TASTY, BUT I HAVE NO IDEA HOW TO UNLOCK A CAR DOOR WITH ONE.

As you know, if you don't like the results of a scientific report, especially about what is good for us and what is bad for us...just wait awhile and another scientist will say the opposite. A recent report said that chocolate helps you lose weight. All studies of chocolate should now stop forever. Let's just go with the weight losing chocolate report. But, of course, they also have said recently that sugar, salt and red meat will kill you. I think I'll eat brown meat from now on (except for rare prime rib and steaks). And, I'm pretty sure that the large amount of salt that I eat daily counter balances the large amount of sugar that I eat daily. That's my scientific report. So be it.

We used to hear about the "last meal" of folks about to be executed. How about the last statement? Jesse Joe Hernandez may have set a new record for strangest, or best, or worse "last words." In Huntsville, just before his recent lethal injection overtook him, he yelled, "GO COWBOYS." We've heard of "Dead Man Walking" and maybe "Dead Man Talking." How about "Dead Fan Yelling?"

I like club sandwiches, but I wonder why they are called "club" sandwiches? Maybe a couple of guys were talking and one said, "You know, I really like a sandwich with an extra piece of bread in the middle." The other guy said, "Me too. Let's start a club."

Most of us eat too much from time to time, and obesity is a serious problem. Bars can cut people off from further drinks if they think they have been over-served. What if restaurants could cut people off? What if you ordered a dessert and the waitperson said, "Sorry Sir, I think you've had enough?" Tips would probably go down with the weight.

You have probably noticed that some restaurants offer "pulled pork" sandwiches. When and why did people start pulling pork? How do you pull pork? Why don't they pull chicken or beef or fish? Or broccoli? I'm thinking of creating a new menu item. Pushed pork. I'll just push it on your plate... right next to your pulled potatoes.

If you've got melted chocolate all over your hands, you're eating it too slowly.

Why do we complain about fish tasting fishy? We don't complain about beef tasting beefy or pork tasting porky.

Every now and then a friend and I will be planning to meet for lunch, and I'll say "How about Mexican food," and he'll say, I had Mexican food yesterday. Or he'll say, "How about Chinese food? And I'll say, "I had Chinese food day before yesterday." I got to thinking about that. Most people in Mexico City eat Mexican food everyday, and probably every meal. The same goes for Chinese folks. Factory workers in Beijing aren't getting hamburgers or tacos at lunch hour. So buck up. You can eat Mexican food two days in a row.

A friend said that he was going to open a new restaurant in Waco and call it "I Don't Care." When folks were planning where to go for lunch or dinner, one would ask, "Where do you want to go?" The other person would say, "I don't care."

CHAPTER FIVE

Waco

There was a local car dealer's promotion recently that advertised a "Bank Reduction Sale." What does that mean? If you buy a car does a bank get smaller? Are banks too fat? Maybe it's a good idea. Waco has more banks per capita than anywhere on earth. Waco has something like 15 independent banks and more coming. If it weren't for banks, dollar stores and Mexican restaurants, Waco could be a semi-ghost town.

One of the great things that Waco has (besides banks, dollar stores and Mexican restaurants) is the Texas Rangers. We have the state's largest Texas Ranger headquarters located right here on the banks of the Brazos, and they're building a new facility that will have space for a lot of wonderful educational activities for Texas school kids. I had the opportunity to go to a Texas Ranger reunion dinner a while back. (I should have had the summer-straw white hat concession.) I was seated near a group of active Ranger Captains who were presenting awards to retired Rangers. These are serious looking law enforcement officials. As I was watching, one of the Ranger Captains alerted, (kind of like a bird dog) kneeled down, raised his pants leg and reached into his boot. I thought,

"My God, he's going for his gun!" But he was really going for his cell phone. When he finished his conversation, his phone was re-booted.

There are some news items that you just couldn't make up. It was reported that a Waco Federal Bureau of Investigation agent plead guilty to killing his neighbor's three pound Mexican Chihuahua by shooting it with a pellet gun. As an aside, it speaks well of his FBI firearms training that he could hit a small moving target with a pellet gun, but seriously...what was he thinking? How dangerous could the dog have been? Did he think it might have been a terrorist from across the border? Generally, Chihuahua's aren't too threatening. They're not like miniature Pit Bulls or anything. What a sad way to end your career. He could have used his skill wisely and gone after Grackles.

I think that this is the second time in my life that I have needed to write the word "Chihuahua." I had and have no idea how to spell "Chihuahua" and if you can't get close to the correct spelling of a word, it's very difficult and time consuming to find it in the dictionary. It is in there. If you're looking, I'll save you some time. It's right after the word "chigoe" which is a tropical flea that you might find on a Chihuahua if you're ever in the tropics with a Chihuahua, which you probably won't be anytime soon but if you are, watch out for those tropical FBI agents.

Where is Capistrano? I don't know exactly, but it does seem to be a big deal when the Swallows come back there. OK, I looked it up on the internet. (Why does my spell-check want me to capitalize "internet"? Is it like a state or a day of the week?) Capistrano is really San Juan Capistrano in California and the Swallows come back there every March 19th, like clockwork. Where do they go in the meanwhile and why isn't it a big deal when they get there?

Swallows are apparently not too adventurous. They could go back to Disneyland or the Grand Canyon or Las Vegas or Crawford, but no, they go back every single year to a mission in Capistrano. Maybe they left something there?

Anyway, everyone has heard of Capistrano because the Swallows do return there. I bet it's a big deal for tourists. Folks probably come from around the world to see the Swallows return. This is not too tough on the good folks of Capistrano. They do nothing but wait around, (the dumb birds do all the work) but Capistranians get all the tourist bucks.

Eureka! Tourist bucks. What's good for San Juanian Capistranians should be good for Wacoans. But Jack, you say, we don't have Swallows...or,

if we ever did have swallows, they left and went back to Capistrano.
But, I say, when it comes to birds you have to think outside of the cage.
We may not have Swallows, but we do have Grackles and Egrets.

When The Grackles Come Back To Waco. When The Egrets Return
To Elm Mott. Can't you just see the traffic backed up on I-35?
Of course you can. It's always backed up.

How exactly do you celebrate the Return Of The Grackles? Every
charitable organization in the city could have a giant car wash. (That's
where you wash giant cars.) Wacoans could be washing cars from Austin,
Dallas and Beyond. (To get to Beyond, go to Lubbock and turn left.)

Maybe if the traffic on I-35 is backed up enough, we could just wash
the cars in place. They wouldn't even have to hit the exit ramps. The Annual
I-35 Waco Drive-By Grackle Sighting and Car Wash. Waco Chamber, are
you listening? You need to get on top of this Grackle opportunity.
It's certainly better than being underneath the Grackle opportunity.

A very unusual event occurred in downtown Waco recently. The
ground was covered with snow in just a few places. Mostly under trees. Oh,
never mind., it wasn't snow, it was grackles. The first person to find a good
use for grackle guano will retire rich.

One of Waco's treasures is the mammoth site that is so unique and
scientifically remarkable. The Mammoth Site is a very interesting place
to visit. There is speculation about what actually killed the mammoths.
They were suddenly trapped and forever frozen in something. Maybe
an advertising promotion could say, "Frozen in Time. Frozen in Slime."
Well, maybe not. Anyway, what were the mammoths stuck in? There are
several viable options. It might have been an early Waco sinkhole. It might
have been an instant algae bloom at Lake Waco. But my best guess is that
after a hard day of foraging, the mammoth group was resting under a very
large tree. Out of nowhere about a hundred and fifty thousand grackles lit
in the tree and the rest is history. Waco's most famous potential tourist
attraction was created by grackle guano.

We frequently hear about what Waco doesn't have. We don't have
a Foley's. We don't have a Neiman's. We don't have a professional sports
team (unless you count Woodway Little League). We don't have Southwest
Airlines. We don't have a Ruth's Chris or a Papasitas.

Some things we don't have, however, are most wonderful. For
instance, you can drive down every single street in Waco and never chance
upon a dreaded.... Parking Meter. Usually we don't think much about things
that aren't there. But try to find a place to park near the Capitol in Austin,

try to find an available parking meter and enough change to put in it and you will quickly remember how wonderful it is that you can park anywhere in Waco (including the airport) without paying for the privilege.

(I heard about a man who solved the parking crisis in Austin. He bought a

parked car.)

I have a thirty-minute commute to and from work in Waco and listen to a variety of radio stations...Waco, Dallas, Austin. There is one thing that I truly love about Waco radio stations and therefore I love about Waco its-own-self. There are no traffic reports! One of my life goals is to never live in a place that has traffic reports. I have children who live in Austin and in the DFW Metro-Mess. They accept not driving while trying to drive. They accept mostly stop and little go. They accept the unacceptable.

Sometimes we Wacoans, Wacoites, Greater Waco Areans (not Aryans), have a complex. We feel put upon by the media. The Rodney Daingerfield of Texas towns. For instance, Texas Monthly won't include us in their "Restaurant Guide" section. They include Galveston, Big Bend, Rio Grande Valley, Beaumont/Port Arthur, Amarillo, Lubbock, and Midland/Odessa. Waco is bigger than Galveston and Big Bend. Waco/Temple/Killeen are bigger than Beaumont/Port Arthur, Lubbock, and Midland/Odessa. I once, years ago while assisting the Waco Chamber, argued with a Texas Monthly staff person about not including Waco. He or she couldn't come up with a good excuse, but eventually said they only include places that Southwest Airlines serves. Of course you can see the logic of tying local restaurants to a Dallas airline. You can't?

Anyway, lately there have been complaints about Waco getting very little positive press about being "near" the Texas White House. Whereas, on the other hand, we got much negative press about the Branch Davidian compound which was near Elk. We don't begrudge Crawford's good fortune, or Elk's not-as-bad-as-it-could-have-been fortune, but why does Waco have to suffer the bad news or the lack of good news? The easiest answer to the problem would be for President Bush to move his ranch to Elk.

Oh well, Waco may be the only US city to be made into a verb. To "Waco" something means to use excessive force to subdue it. Can you think of any other cities that have become verbs? Someone can "go Hollywood" (meaning to act like a movie star) but I think that's an adverb or adjective or maybe a dangling participle. (It's been too long since I had a serious conversation with an English teacher.)

What's in a name? Well, there are 12 peaks in Colorado higher than Pike's Peak. Can you name one? (I made the number 12 up, but it might be close.) Names of places can obviously be important in our ability to remember them and appreciate them. McLennan County has some unusually named places.

Waco, for instance, was named after an Indian tribe. (I'm sorry, a distinguished, like-thinking group of Indigenous/and/or/Native Americans.) Somehow when kids today play "Cowboys and Indigenous Americans," it just doesn't have quite the same ring.)

What about Elm Mott? My dictionary doesn't have the word "mott" in it. It has "motte" which means a hill upon which a castle is built, but not "mott." "Mottle" means a colored spot and I guess that elm leaves have colored spots, but would you name a town after one?

Where in Lacy Lakeview can you get a view of a lake (or a Lacy for that matter)? What does Beverly Hills have in common with the one in California? Speeding tickets? Who was Beverly and where are the hills? (Are those the things that the policemen hide on the other side of?) Is there just one spring in China Spring? And what's Chinese about it? A high MSG level?

Does the town of Tours have any? Did Ross, Leroy, Eddy or Bruce (Bruceville) have last names? Are they temperamental in Moody? Just wondering.

The ACLU or some such organization is suggesting that Los Angeles should change its name because it's too religious. The name, not the city. The City of Angels could become "The City of Those Who Don't Have an Opinion One-way or the Other" or maybe "Los Agnostics" would do. This could start a far-reaching PC trend. We couldn't have St. Louis, or St. Paul, or Falls Church, or even Temple, Texas. It was also suggested that Squaw Valley was derogatory toward Indigenous Americans, who are apparently easily derogated. We would have to change the names of half the towns in Oklahoma. What about Waco? It was named after the Huaco Indians, it's said. I don't know how we know how to spell "Huaco." I'm guessing the Indigenous Americans in question didn't have a written language. So how do we know how to spell Indigenous American names? And of course the Brazos was originally named "Brazos de Dios," translated as "The Arms of God." That's a double whammy. Ethnicity and religion. Surely it must be changed. How about Water River? It's generic and might not offend anyone. How about Water River City for Waco? It could be compelling for tourist. "Come to Water River City and enjoy the lovely Water River". Who could resist?

It was recently reported that the City of Waco was going to annex the McGregor airport. This, of course, seems weird and the annexation rules sound complex. I guess that the City of Waco feels that the addition of the

McGregor airport would add to its property and sales tax base. Once again, I'm afraid, the city is thinking small. What the heck, annex DFW Airport! With the property and sales tax revenue from DFW, Waco could fix the low-water dam and a couple of dozen sidewalks.

If you have driven by Providence Hospital on Hwy. 6 in the last few months and observed the new construction, you may have thought of the Three Little Pigs. Then again, maybe you didn't. You will recall that the Three Little Pigs' Mother told them that they were old enough to move out and take care of themselves. This was probably the most valuable lesson in the fairy tale, at least for parents of teenagers. Anyway, the three pigs left home.

The first little pig built a house made of straw and the Big Bad Wolf huffed and puffed, blew the house down and ate the 1st Little Pig. Fairy tales were not Politically Correct. If written today, the Big Bad Wolf would be an evil Profit Making Businessman and would not eat the Little Pig (just think of the saturated fat), but instead, under threat of prison for air pollution (the blowing straw), would take Sensitivity Training and start a charitable Habitat for Hogs program

The second Little Pig built a house of sticks and suffered the same fate as his brother. Severe baconitis. The three pigs were obviously male. If the three pigs had been female they would still be at home with the Mother Pig looking at fabric swatches and trying to decide whether to paint the living room molding off-white, ivory or ecru.

The third Little Pig built his house of bricks, followed all of the city codes (including the number of trees per parking place) and lived happily ever after. He was such a good example; he got to sit next to the First Lady in the balcony at the State of the Union speech.

Anyway, of the three Providence buildings, one is built of wood, one has metal studs and one is being built of concrete blocks. A very nice Providence employee told me that the three buildings are for three different purposes and have different building code requirements. The mostly wood building will be apartments, the metal stud building will be for assisted living and the concrete building will be a nursing home. Each will withstand the huff and puff test and the Big Bad Code Enforcer.

You can go, while still on the Providence property, from an apartment, to assisted living to a full-scale nursing home. Wonder why they didn't finish the cycle and build a cemetery?

Driving into Kitok's parking lot, a sign said that it is temporarily closed. To my knowledge, this leaves the world totally void of Oriental Fries. This is not acceptable. Surely, if needed, some entrepreneur will fill this void. (I can easily capitalize "Oriental" without even thinking about not capitalizing "French."

Oriental Fries are just one of thousands of things that I can't cook. I can take frozen things and put them in an oven. (Actually, I'm one of the best cooks you ever thaw.) When our kids were little, I used to be the cook on Sunday nights. We had Dad's Sunday Night Supper Surprise. The surprise was if anybody ate anything. Much of the food was unidentifiable. To this day, my three daughters don't eat from Sunday afternoons until Monday mornings. Old habits are hard to break. So was my meatloaf.

NO MORE SWEATING OVER THE HOT STOVE FOR ME. MAYBE JUST PERSPIRING OVER THE MICROWAVE.

In the army we were told that enlisted men sweat, officers perspire and officers' wives "glow". I have an inherited condition in which my forehead sweats without much provocation. (My Dad's forehead used to break out in a sweat when he ate Mexican food.) When asked why my forehead sweats so freely, my wife says it's due to the fat content.

Recently someone who has probably forgotten more about urban planning that I would ever know mentioned a serious problem with Downtown Waco. He said that there were too many parking spaces. My first thought was that this was a typo or a September April Fool's joke, but he was serious. He explained that many parking areas were under-utilized and could be filled up with retail type businesses and then people could and should walk to these places instead of driving to them. I guess like 6th Street in Austin or the West End in Dallas. But I'm not sure where they are going to be walking from. They aren't going to walk from Hewitt or Lake Air or even Baylor to downtown Waco. So we will need a large parking lot for them to drive to where they can leave their cars and then walk to downtown. Or maybe instead of building a new parking lot to walk from, we could just use the existing parking areas and build retail places in the existing empty buildings. Maybe.

Did you see the picture in last month's Wacoan of former Baylor President Dr. Robert Sloan? When he was in Waco, I'd swear he had straight brown hair. In the picture he now has curly gray hair. I'm guessing that the Houston traffic turned him gray and the Houston humidity turned him curly.

Maybe the Waco Chamber could use this as a selling point. "Waco...Better Here...Better Hair." But there may be an even better new chamber slogan. I met a new friend recently who told me how much he and his family enjoyed living in Waco, which had surprised them. He said, "Waco is like a fungus. It grows on you." So there, Waco Chamber. Scrap the "We Do" logo and go with "Waco, Fungus Capitol of Texas"...or maybe "Waco. There's a Fungus Among Us."

I saw, a while back, that country music star, Pat Green, was going to perform in Waco. His concert was at a local club on a Tuesday night starting at 10pm. I said to Vicki that it seemed that that would cut a lot of people out, being that late on a week night. She said, "Maybe they don't want any old people there." I guess she was right. I'm not much of a namedropper and I've never met Pat Green, but I do know his nice Waco Mom, Patty.

A headline in the Waco Trib said, "Complex auction attracts no takers." Well, maybe they should have made it less complex. (I know, I know. It was about an apartment complex, but still...).

In case you're counting...another great thing about Waco is that there is no Occupy Waco group. At least I haven't smelled one. What a bunch of crazies these folks are. Have you seen the videos in which a speaker says a few words and the crowd repeats in unison everything that is said? Have you seen where they approve something by waving their fingers upright and disapprove by waving their fingers downward. ("Downright" is a good word, but isn't the opposite of "upright".) Some of these folks should have stayed in kindergarten. They could protest naptime by waving their fingers downright.

As I drive around Waco, I don't slow down for speed bumps. It might encourage them. And speaking of driving, it might be a good idea for AA and AAA to offer combined memberships (AAAAA). That way, if you fall off the wagon, they can tow you home.

CHAPTER SIX

Marlin

I was raised (I never liked the word "reared") in Marlin, which is the county seat of Falls County, about 28 miles southeast of Waco. Way back at the turn of the century (the previous one) Marlin was a famous health center. Hot mineral water from artesian wells was discovered and in 1900 the first hotel and bathhouse were built. People came from all over the country to bathe in the hot, stinky and foul tasting water. Passenger trains would offload tourists and local merchant representatives (called Barkers) would compete to take them to local boarding houses and hotels. Marlin became a training site for major league baseball teams. The first was the Chicago White Sox in 1903 followed by the Philadelphia Phillies, the Cincinnati Red and the St. Louis Browns. They all stayed at the Arlington Hotel. The New York Giants under John J. McGraw made Marlin their permanent spring training camp in 1908 and built a large ballpark with grandstands and bleachers and played exhibition games with teams from all around.

Marlin remained an active health center for many years and still has an excellent hospital today. My paternal grandfather (who died before I was born) was a doctor in Marlin and my father was a doctor in Marlin.

My maternal grandfather taught agriculture classes in Marlin High School & his wife, my maternal grandmother, was one of the first female school principals in the state. For some reason there used to be County School Superintendents and I'm told that she was the first female one elected in the state. My mother was a home economics teacher at Marlin High School. My father's sister taught history at Marlin High School and one of my mother's sisters was, for a time, an elementary librarian in Marlin.

So I come from a line of physicians and educators, and I never had any interest in being either one. When I was a young boy, my brother and I would sometimes go with my Dad to his office in the hospital, if he needed to catch up on paperwork after hours. I never liked the anesthetic smell and I hated getting shots. I didn't like doctors in their workplace. My older brother and I did have fun playing with wheel chairs in the empty halls of the clinic.

Marlin was a great place to grow up. Most everyone says that about their hometowns, but it was true of Marlin for those of my generation. Everything, from schools to churches to businesses were positive influences on young folks. We had a great life.

Things have changed. Small towns without industries are very hard pressed to keep up with the costs of everything that it takes to run a town and you just can't compete with the opportunities of larger cities. Kids leave after high school and don't come back.

It's sad, but true that the wonderful small town life of the good old days are probably gone forever.

Random thoughts about Marlin and Falls County

I've mentioned before the terrible state of repair of the streets in my hometown of Marlin. It's, as it always is, a matter of money. There just isn't enough and probably never will be. Sometimes it seems our streets are paved with "good intensions."

Driving in Marlin is one continual obstacle course. You have to plan your trips across town in advance to avoid the really big potholes. If the city had any money, which it doesn't, I would consider suing it for a new malady it has created, Shaken Adult Syndrome.

The good news is that we don't have any drive-by-shootings. It would be virtually impossible to fire a weapon out of a car bouncing like a washing machine on a trampoline.

After one cow (a Canadian import) was found to have Mad Cow Disease in Washington state or somewhere in the upper-left USA, some bureaucrats have decided that every one of the zillions of cows in the USA should have a computer chip inserted under its skin so that every cow can be traced and it's location monitored. I guess that there would be more "cow-scans" than "cat-scans." Logical thinking persons might consider this an excessive response to a so-far minor problem. Cattlemen (male cattlepersons) such as those in Falls County have stronger views.

I was standing in line behind a couple of cowboys at a convenience store in Marlin when one suggested that, "They oughta put them computer chips under the skin of lawyers and politicians so we see where they are." The other suggested that the chip be like an electric dog collar wherein you could shock em when you wanted to. There are many more cows in this country than lawyers and politicians. The economics of the situation is on the side of the cowboys' idea.

Speaking of Falls County, in Marlin there are frequent boil orders due to problems with the antiquated water system. It's easy to buy a gallon of water at the grocery store for cooking, but I'm not ever sure about the ice in the icemaker. Should you boil the ice before you use it?

I have a friend who lives in Marlin, but on the edge of town where there are woods and ravines and things that appeal to a variety of animals. This causes problems. Skunks are occasionally a problem, and when skunks are a problem, they're a serious problem. The little stinkers. But lately, some varmint has been coming into their yard at night and eating the flowers in their flower garden. As a part-time, amateur, unskilled, half-baked gardener myself, I can understand the amount of frustration that would occur if some uninvited guest destroyed all of your hard work. So, my friend decided he had to take action. He said he had gotten a trap. What kind, I asked? A "Have-A-Heart" trap, he said. That's the kind that allows the animal to enter the trap for food and then they can't get back out. It's a "humanitarian" trap. So, I asked, what will you do when you catch the varmint? He said, "I'll shoot him." Sometimes that "have-a-heart deal" only goes so far.

Why do we want to treat animals in a "humanitarian" way? Why not treat them in an "animalitarian" way? We generally treat our pets better than our in-laws, who are for the most part human.

I read that because an increasing number of people are having heart attacks while on vacation, big, expensive hotels are now equipped with sophisticated defibrillators. They are computer-controlled to deliver the exact electric shock needed to revive a heart attack victim. That's in expensive hotels. At motels in Marlin, they just drag you across the carpet and touch your finger to the doorknob.

Someone once got a speeding ticket outside of Marlin, and was very upset and wanted to do something immediately. He pulled into the first filling station he could find and asked the man behind the counter if there was a criminal lawyer in town. The local replied, "Well, there's a couple of them that we're suspicious of, but we can't ever prove nothing on em."

CHAPTER SEVEN

Family

Vicki, Jack, Dogs and Cats

Vicki and I were married in 1966 in Waco. We had a limited, expense regulated honeymoon in Austin. We came home a day early from the trip because we spent our money on a dog. Someone had mentioned to us, before we tied the knot, that dogs were a very cohesive factor in a marriage. We figured we needed all the cohesion we could get, so we got a dog. We named him Charmin, so that no one would squeeze him. He was a Wired Haired Terrier and a pretty good dog. He was the first of many dogs in our family.

After 5 years or so, we had our first daughter, Sarah. Sarah was born, while we were in the Army, at Darnell Army Hospital at Ft. Hood. We still have the bill from that childbirth. It was for $5.25. Vicki and Sarah were in the hospital for a little less than 24 hours. The Army was tough on Army wives too. The bill was $1.75 for each meal that Vicki was served while in the hospital. She really only got two meals, but we decided that it wasn't worth it to fight the overcharge. It's amazing what a great childbirth experience and child you can have for $5.25.

Our little-middle child Claire was born on New Years Day in 1974 in Waco. There was a very odd coincidence that our new health insurance (after leaving the Army) kicked in on that very day. So we missed the tax deduction, but came out way ahead with the insurance.

Thirteen months later. Lauren was born in Waco. Lauren and Claire were frequently more like twins than non-twins. In high school, they looked alike and people were frequently confused about which was which, and they enjoyed purposely confusing people.

Today, all three girls are doing exceptionally well. Sarah is married to Ted and she is a medical administrator and computer whiz. Claire, a Speech Pathologist, is married to Gavin and they have our two oldest grandchildren, Caroline and Jack. Lauren, a non-practicing attorney (my favorite kind), is married to Matt and they have three children, John Matthew and twins, Connor and Luke.

We have truly been blessed with a wonderful family and extended family.

My wife Vicki sometimes has random thoughts. She asked recently if there were male ladybugs. This came up because our grand granddaughter, Caroline, got a bugarium as a gift. It's like an aquarium, but you put bugs in it instead of fish. I'm not sure who decided that young children want to capture, feed and watch bugs. Most little girls I've known were not interested in getting up-close and personal with bugs. They wanted to get down-far and impersonal with bugs. Screaming comes to mind.

Anyway, Vicki captured a ladybug to keep for Caroline, so we now have a temporary, homemade mini-bugarium at our house. But anyway, it's a good question. Are there male ladybugs? The answer is...yes, but they don't like to talk about it. Male ladybugs are very self-conscience. Gender related questions really bug them.

Vicki and I are different in many things. There may be something to that "opposites attract" deal. She, for instance believes in doing everything exactly right. I believe in doing things about half right and then taking a TV break. Or maybe just taking a TV break without doing anything else before or after. I was thinking that there should be a good name for my condition, besides "lazy slacker." So, after giving it some thought, I've decided that I'm an "Imperfectionist." That doesn't sound so bad, does it?

Recently, I was acting naturally (being an imperfectionist) and postponing a honey-do when Vicki gave me her Nike stare. The one that says, "Just Do It!"

We have two daughters that live in the Frisco area and one in Austin. They have all adjusted to the big cities. The Dallas/Fort Worth area, also known as the MetroMess is unique. My wife was driving alone in the Greater (than what?) Dallas area recently, not anywhere close to Highland Park, and stopped for gas. A beggar (is there a PC term for beggars? Challenged loan applicants?) approached Vicki as she began to pump gas, to ask for money. The very first words out of his mouth were, "Don't shoot me!" He had apparently heard about the concealed-carry gun law, and hey, you can't be too safe these days. Vicki could easily have been a Pistol Packing Mama. Convinced that she was unarmed, he then went on to explain that he lived in Houston but was "stranded" in Dallas and needed $38 for a bus ticket. The bus ticket's actual cost was $39, but he already had $1which he was unselfishly willing to invest in the venture. About the time he finished his story the owner of the filling-station (they can't be called "service" stations anymore) came out to rescue his customer. While English was not his 1st, 2nd, 3rd or 4th language, he did convince the Houstonian to move on through hand jesters and an obvious sincerity. Vicki tried to thank him for coming to her rescue, but wasn't sure he understood the Central Texas language. He could count US money.

Vicki does most of the driving in our family. I sit behind the wheel, but you know...

Vicki was recently shopping in a Waco grocery store. She had a bunch of bananas (how many bananas are in a bunch?) in her selections. When checking out the items, the clerk said that her fruit-weigher-thingy was not working so Vicki could not have the bananas and the clerk put them aside. Vicki was shocked into speechlessness (a most rare occurrence) and left without her bananas. Yes, we have no bananas. But we do have store clerks with the IQ and adaptability of a banana. (After this item appeared in the magazine, the Waco manager of HEB called me to be sure that it wasn't his store that was banana free. It wasn't.)

Vicki left me a sarcastic note the other day saying that I should try out for "American Idle." Well, the jokes on her because she misspelled "Idol." Uh, never mind.

You know you've had too much company or too much food if you have to run your dishwasher 3 times in one day, which we did on Easter. Vicki likes for me to dress in white, cause she thinks the dishwasher should match the stove and refrigerator.

Wives frequently don't appreciate the various talents of their husbands. I realize that this is not a news flash, but here's a good example. Vicki doesn't appreciate my exceptional talent at "trash balancing."

Other people might look at the trashcan in our pantry and decide that it is completely full and can't possibly hold anymore and should be taken out. Well, after years of practice, I can balance an incredible amount of additional trash on top of the stack. Empty 2-liter bottles tend to want to roll off and it's in just such situations that my remarkable skill comes into play. Trash balancing is a completely unappreciated art form. At least at my house. Maybe if it were an Olympic event, my skills would be more appreciated. If they can have synchronized swimming, ice dancing and the hammer throw, surely they can have trash balancing. I think I've got a real shot at trash balancing gold.

Halloween came and went and we had some really great Halloween candy this year. Unfortunately, we ran out early. Looking back, we probably should have saved some for the kids.

Now Thanksgiving has come and gone. I love turkey and dressing. I prefer dark meat, which there appears to be less of per turkey each year, and Vicki makes the best dressing in the world. I don't know why we don't eat this great meal every week or month rather than once or twice a year. I would be thankful again and again.

Speaking of favorite meals, they say that breakfast is the most important meal of the day, but I haven't eaten breakfast in the last 40 years or so. The reason is not a big secret. I just can't eat on an empty stomach.

My wife, Vicki, is a bag lady. She always has bags of stuff to take with her wherever she goes. Once I planned to write a book entirely about the things in her bags, but I figured out it wouldn't work. The age of the great epics is past.

Vicki and I were talking about planting some additional winter flowers in our garden. I wonder if the other flowers make fun of pansies?

You may have seen a recent news item from Bates Township, Michigan. *Man shot by cat.* Michigan State Police said that the cat-owner was cooking his dinner when his cat, who was meandering along his countertop, knocked a 9mm loaded handgun onto the floor, discharging the weapon and shooting the man in the leg. I'm not sure if this was a catastrophe or a cataclysm, but I know it wasn't dogmatic. This would have never happened with a dog. Dogs don't jump five times their height to get to places they shouldn't be.

I'm a dog person. There was probably a dog in my house when I was born, and there almost always has been since. As a dedicated dog person,

I've never really cared much for cats. They never cared much for me either. A few months ago a cat moved into our yard. She delighted in driving our dog crazy by preening on the other side of the glass door. Soon, my kindhearted wife bought cat food and began feeding the trespasser. Very soon we had two cats living in our yard and garage and on top of our cars. (Even when it's dry, the clever cats can find some mud to make tracks on my windshield.) They are now permanent. One of them is a little skittish, the other if very friendly and playful. Her favorite game is walking under your feet and trying to trip you to make you fall and break your arm or your head. It's great cat fun. Vicki thought that the cats needed names, so I finally named them. They are "GetOuttaTheWay" and "YouToo". Cats don't really need names, cause they don't come when you call them.

109

If cats could talk, I think they would lie to you.

Of the dozens of dogs I my life, the best one was Scruffy. Scruffy was a mutt and was named Scruffy because he was. Scruffy was run over by a car and had to have his right rear leg amputated. We never told him about the lost leg, so he didn't seem to know it was gone. He could run, jump (not on counters) and play as before. He adjusted very well. When our girls were small, we used to enter chili cook offs and cook chili. Scruffy always went with us. We had a little booth or stand and our sign said "Dog's Leg Chili." People would look at the sign and then look at Scruffy and then look at us a little strangely. We never won a prize. Was it the chili or the name? (It was the chili.)

My current dog wants me to throw the Frisbee to him, but he doesn't really want to bring it back. It's a playing problem. I guess you might call it a "Fetch 22."

Why is it that 95% of married people, both men and women, say they get along better with their spouse's Mother-In-Law than they do their own?

I TOLD VICKI THAT I HAD GIVEN IT A LOT OF THOUGHT AND I HAD DECIDED THAT I MIGHT WANT TO BE CREMATED. SHE SAID, "OK, LET'S GO."

Vicki bought some Ezekiel Bread upon the recommendation of a friend. The bread is from a recipe in Ezekiel, chapter 4, verse 9. The bread tastes kind of like it's thousands of years old but without the flavor.

Speaking of eating, in the summer at our house, we eat a ton of tomatoes. I eat them with every meal and sometimes between meals.

We grow some and buy some from Cedar Springs, which are the best in the whole world. Tomatoes are said to be a cancer fighter. I will never get cancer in the summer.

Speaking of food, I recently tried to tell Vicki which spices I thought she should use in a vegetable recipe, but she didn't want my sage advice. Vicki once told me that if I wanted breakfast in bed, I'd have to sleep in the kitchen.

A friend told me recently that he was getting hard of hearing. Wonder where that phrase originated? I hear pretty well. Am I soft of hearing? Vicki would disagree that I hear well. She keeps complaining that I never listen to her. Or something like that.

Vicki and I enjoy having an attractive yard. We concentrate on our back yard which almost no one ever sees other than us. We till, we plant, we water, we weed, we mulch, we water, we weed, we water, we weed. We enjoy our garden, but I can't say we enjoy gardening. It is hard, hot, and frequently boring work. We enjoy the result, but getting there is not half the fun.

When I was trimming the limbs of some trees in the yard... I got out my step-ladder, cause I don't relate well with my real ladder.

Vicki and I were involved in a petty argument that had gone on too long. To end the mini-crisis, I said, "OK, I'll admit I'm wrong if you'll admit I'm right." She agreed and insisted that I go first. I said, "OK, I'm wrong," She quickly said, "You're right!"

We've talked before about how careful you have to be in the grocery store these days or you will wind up with the wrong product. Like instead of Classic Coke, you get home with some undrinkable Cherry, Vanilla, Lime and Berry Swill Coke. Vicki, in anticipation of visiting grandchildren bought a six-pack of little ready made Jell-O packages. The way-too-small print said "Sugar-Free". Wow! Sugar-free Jell-O tastes just like cardboard. Without the texture.

It was obviously Vicki's fault. It's so easy to blame others. That's why I enjoy doing it.

Vicki and I had the opportunity recently to go on a quick cruise out of Galveston. On the bus from the parking lot to the dock, I noticed that many of the folks, based on their appearance, seemed to be going on the cruise just for the food. I said to myself, "Please God, don't let them have a bathing suit."

My prayer was not answered. Modesty is a forgotten virtue. I saw more exposed skin than a leather tanner.

They say that power in the wrong hands can be a very serious problem. That's why I keep my fist clenched tightly around the TV remote.

An organization of which Vicki is a member recently gave its members aprons. It's a nice apron, but what do you do with it? When was the last time you saw someone wearing an apron at your house. I'm guessing that women (certainly not men) wore aprons because they were always fooling with flower and grease and things were flying around the kitchen. When I cut open a frozen package and put the contents in the microwave or the oven, my clothes really don't need much protection. On the other hand when I'm eating the prepared food, then I may need an apron. But hey, I look good in anything I eat.

Last month I mentioned the decline of aprons in our society. I got two nice emails from two nice ladies who said that my report of the death of aprons was premature. One of the ladies, who had moved here in the last couple of years from California, said that aprons were making a comeback and were kind of trendy, with designer aprons appearing. She said that she had a collection of about twenty aprons. Another lady correctly informed me that aprons were not to protect your clothes from "flower," but from "flour." Picky, picky, picky. One could be cooking with flowers. There's cornflower, dill, fennel, lemon verbena, mint, rosemary and squash blossom among others. (You'll notice that the edible flowers are listed in alphabetical order, just as I found them on the internet page about edible flowers.) And I guess aprons could protect your clothes from flour also.

Vicki recently interrupted my TV watching in my very comfortable recliner with an unsolicited suggestion that she thought I might be able to make some money as a model for an "Inaction Figure". It's tough to get a good wife. For all she knew, I could have been practicing meditation. I do practice meditation sometimes. It's better than just sitting around and doing nothing. I overheard Vicki talking to a friend about the "overstuffed recliner". Turns out she wasn't talking about my chair. One Sunday after lunch, Vicki asked, "What are you going to do today?" I said, "Nothing." She said, "That's what you did yesterday." I said, "Yeah, but I didn't finish."

You may have seen the infomercial or ad on TV about that grass, grown from strange looking blue seeds, that will grow anywhere. The ad says, and it shows a picture, that the grass will grow on concrete. I'm not going to get any, cause Vicki and I looked all over our modest estate and we can't find a single place where we want to grow grass on our concrete.

Sometimes one gets an early indication of how the marriage is going to go. At my wedding the preacher said to Vicki, "Do you take this man to be your lawfully wedded husband?" She said, "I do." He then turned to me and said, "Do you take this woman to be your lawfully wedded wife?" Vicki said, "He does."

Eating habits with families have changed a lot from the old days till now. In the old days, the mother rang a dinner bell to call the family to dinner. In today's young families, the mother calls the family to dinner by saying, "OK, everybody get in the car."

So Vicki was filling out a form at a doctor's office. It asked who should be notified in case of an emergency. She put my name down. Then it asked what the relationship was. She put down that I was her Insignificant Other. It's tough getting a good wife.

Here's a tip for you guys who are looking for that perfect gift for the wife or girl friend or co-worker or niece or cousin or sister-in-law, or mother-in-law or any other female kinda significant other. I gave Vicki an amulet for Christmas. It worked like a charm!

While driving into a small town recently (Frost, Texas, home of the Frost Polar Bears) I was stopped by a local gendarme for going 55 in a 45 mile-an-hour speed trap. This is only the 3rd speeding ticket I've gotten in about 50 years of driving. All three of them would have been overlooked by a commonsensical, compassionate law enforcement person, but the local cop in Frost showed no compassion at all. He hardly even spoke. He didn't even ask for proof of insurance. He took my drivers license and came back a couple of minutes later with my $155 ticket. He didn't want to discuss any other options. The odd thing about him was that he had a great Elvis impersonation going on. Long black hair with big, thick mutton chops. The sad thing was that he was doing a great impersonation of the old, fat Elvis. If you're going to do Elvis...do the young handsome Elvis.

We all know that men are better drivers than women. Vicki, for instance, can't drive worth a flip. The fact that after 40 something years of driving she has never had a ticket of any kind, or a wreck doesn't count. She did get a ticket once for not having on her seat belt. She was riding in the front seat passenger seat while another lady was driving in a parade. The JP tore up the ticket based on the stupidity of the police person and the fact that he looked nothing like Elvis.

There are a lot of changes in the automobile industry these days. My Dad always wanted to own a Cadillac, but never did. He usually had Oldsmobiles, which were very nice cars. Vicki and I were in the Army in the early 70's (actually, I was in the Army and Vicki was just along for the fun) and decided to buy a new car. We went to a Pontiac dealer near Ft. Hood and were dead-set on buying a nice economical family car. But, with the help of an effective salesperson, we could not resist the allure of a brand new Grand-Prix. It was kind of beige and had a darker top and it was one hot car. We thoroughly enjoyed it for several years. Now, of course there are no Oldsmobile's and soon will be no Pontiacs. The times they are a changing.

I'm sure it was Vicki's decision to buy the Grand-Prix. When we were first married, we made a deal. I'd make all of the major decision and she'd make the minor ones. It's worked really well. In 40 years of marriage, we haven't had a major decision come up yet.

Actually, Vicki will do absolutely anything I want her to do for me. Of course, she's the one who decides what it is that I want her to do for me.

I recently got a new used car. Vicki asked if it had heated seats. I think it does. I found a button for "rear defroster."

Sometimes it may seem that I don't give my wife, Vicki, credit for her intelligence and unusual philosophical insights. (OK, OK so I don't ever give her credit.) But occasionally, she will turn into a regular Plato or Socrates or some other long-dead person who ate a lot of Greek food with a lot of crummy tasting curry on it. Vicki is not exactly a sports fan. Other than the grandchildren's soccer or T-Ball games, she'd just as soon not pay any attention at all. Recently when I was watching the National Championship NCAA baseball game with my Orange & White heroes, (I've forgotten exactly how the game turned out) she wandered in for about 3 minutes to watch. And after watching the game for just those 3 minutes, she came up with one of the great philosophical and weighty questions in the wide world of sports. She simply asked, "Why do baseball players spit?"

This is a question for the ages. Why do baseball players spit? Basketball players don't spit. Football players don't spit (unless they have grass in their mouths). Volleyball players don't spit. Golfers and tennis players don't spit. Why baseball? It may be because baseball is the only sport where the players eat during the game. They chew tobacco, they eat sunflower seeds, chew gum and probably have some cheese fondue in the dugout that you can't see from here. This is not a totally valid excuse, however. I eat two or three times a day and never feel the compulsion to spit. I wonder if baseball fields ever have a problem with sunflowers growing in the infield? With all of those seeds being spit around, you'd wonder why not. So the real answer to the question of why do baseball players spit is... I don't know.

Vicki was laid up for a couple of weeks recently following foot surgery. At the end of those two weeks I heard it reported that there had been a precipitous drop in consumer spending in the US. I apologize for any drop in your 401K, but she's back out there shopping again, so it will all be better soon.

I probably shouldn't have mentioned that and I'll probably be told so. But here is some good advice for married men. You should just forget all of your mistakes. There's no use in two people remembering the same things... forever and ever and ever.

If I ever get the urge to get in touch with my feminine side, I think I'll just misplace my car keys or cell phone.

Vicki once said she thought I suffered from "Attention Defi. Something." I didn't really catch it. I was thinking about a chicken fried steak at the time.

I told Vicki I was considering giving up my day job to pursue a career in comedy. She said, "You can't possibly be serious!" I knew I'd have her support.

I was looking in our bedroom mirror and said, "I look terrible. I look old, bald, overweight and ugly. I really need you to pay me a compliment." Vicki said, "Your eyesight's still good." It's really tough to get a good wife.

Vicki is allergic to wheat products, and tries to avoid them, but sometimes eats them anyway. I think she's gluten for punishment.

Speaking of eating meals, if you eat a late breakfast and/or early lunch, it's called "brunch." But what if you eat a late lunch or early supper (or dinner)? Shouldn't that be called a "lupper" or a "linner?"

A relative recently had an unusual experience. This is an almost totally true story, just like all of my other stories. There was one of those rented storerooms in a kind of un-traveled area and some of a grandmother's furniture and stuff was stored there after she went to a nursing home. The storeroom owner called to say that the storeroom had been broken into and was unlocked. The relative immediately went to the site where it was discovered that nothing, absolutely nothing, had been stolen. Apparently the thieves weren't into granny furniture. Doesn't look too promising for the garage sale.

We (that means Vicki) decided that we needed a new breakfast room table and chairs, so we (Vicki) found a new home for our old table and chairs. Our breakfast room now has a card table in it while we shop for a new table. Vicki has a very specific table that she's looking for. It's the kind that nobody has. She has looked at most of the furniture stores in North America in person or on-line with no luck. There was one store that she hadn't been to yet, so I decided that I would go look. I was shocked to find out that 90% of the new dining room/breakfast room tables in stores today are "counter-height". That means that when you sit in one of the chairs, your feet won't reach the floor, not even if you're a tall person, which we aren't. You have to either dangle you feet like a puppet or put them awkwardly on a cross bar on the bottom part of the chair. Why in the world would someone want a dining room chair from which your feet won't reach the floor? If you have a "sit-down dinner", wouldn't you want to sit down with your feet on the floor and relax? Maybe it's about the eternal search for youth. We want to get back in high-chairs.

I was recently reminded of a true story that happened a few years ago. There was an older gentleman (even older than I am) in Marlin also named Jack Smith. He died. He had been a golfer. A week or so after his death, Vicki answered the phone one day and a guy, who (should that be whom?) Vicki didn't know, asked if he might be able to buy Mr. Smith's golf clubs. Vicki stammered a minute and said, "Well, he hardly ever plays, but I don't know if he wants to sell his clubs." There was a long pause on the other end and the guy said he thought he must have the wrong number. He did. The surprising thing about the situation is that Vicki didn't go ahead and sell my clubs on the spot to gain more room in the closet for her shoes.

We recently took a vacation up the East Coast including Canada. We visited Quebec. (The locals call it "Kee-beck." It seems strange that those folks don't know how to pronounce their own town's name.) Quebec is a fascinating and beautiful European-like city. They had some amazing shops including lots of art galleries with really nice art. Some of the paintings that I admired were very expensive, in the range of $5,000 to $8,000. I was surprised to see that the price tags had the regular price and then also a price for 12 payments or 24 payments or 36 payments. Fine art on the installment plan. I wondered what kind of repossession plan they have if that 34th payment didn't come in.

The vacation was a cruise on the upper East coast. Cruises feature two main activities. Eating and trying to find your way back to your cabin. I ate too much, and enjoyed it too much and gained too much weight. Vicki said that when I die, she was going to donate my body to science fiction.

Vicki reminded me that in the old days, some guy named Morse invented the telegraph. It was a wonderful new means of communicating with people far away. You typed (tapped the keys) and your message came out the other end like magic. We have come a long, long way, baby. Now we tap our keys and the message comes out at the other end like magic and we call it texting. Amazing progress.

In the old days, we had party lines, where a group of different people shared the same telephone number and could pick up their phone and listen the other folk's conversations and know what their friends and neighbors were doing. Now we have Facebook. Amazing progress.

A friend emailed me what was called The Joke of the Year. Here it is. "Two women were sitting quietly together, minding their own business." No Vicki, I don't think that's funny.

I recently overheard Vicki telling a friend that I was a model husband. Later, I told her that that was an awfully nice thing to say. She told me to look up the word "model." I did. The dictionary said "model" means, "a small imitation of the real thing." Gee thanks.

I recently asked Vicki what she liked most about me...my good looks or my superior intellect? She said, "Your sense of humor."

Parents

Nostalgia, as someone said, isn't what it used to be. I've had reason lately to think about my parents, both deceased. We are never too far from the parents who molded us.

My Dad, who died way too young, some 43 years ago, was a stickler (an increasingly rare phenomenon) for proper grammar and use of the English language. He instantly corrected my brother and me whenever we misspoke. I was reminded of this while watching a television commercial for Tony Sanchez who was running for Governor. In the commercial, Mr. Sanchez's daughter says about her father, "He taught my brothers and I..."

Well, I'm not sure what he taught them, but it wasn't grammar. We need more sticklers and more alert video producers.

I was thinking about my mother the other day when someone mentioned eating "dinner." My mom, and I guess a lot of Central Texas ladies of her generation, always called the noon meal "dinner" and the evening meal "supper." Well, now we generally consider the noon meal "lunch" and the evening meal "dinner." The dictionary defines "dinner" as the principal meal of the day, so it could be either time. "Supper" is defined as the evening meal when dinner is taken at midday. In my childhood, the noon meal was probably the big meal of the day, so I guess my mom was right. But what about "breakfast?" I'm assuming that we "fast" during the night and then we "break" this "fast" when we eat our first meal of the day and therefore we have "breakfast." Maybe we could call the evening meal "startfast" and we could forget the dinner/supper confusion.

Children

One of my daughters in the MetroMess area recently moved to a new abode. Her new street is named "Diablo Grande." Strange name for a street. It roughly translates as "Big Devil." So my granddaughter, The Little Angel, now lives on Big Devil street.

One of my lovely daughters recently brought a couch to our house. She had no room for it and thought that we might. If you get furniture from your children, is it a "hand-me-up?"

Speaking of daughters, while ours were home for the holidays, we had a dinner table discussion about where exactly one should place silverware on the plate when finished eating. The consensus was that if the plate is like a clock face, the knife and fork should start in the middle of the plate and point outward and over the edge of the plate and should point to 4:20. I was for three thirty, but was out-voted. The next time I win an argument with my wife and daughters will be the first time.

For a great Mother's Day present, our sweet daughters and their semi-sweet husbands (kind of like chocolate) came home for a weekend project of texturing and repainting our dining room. It was a great idea that they had and we had a great family time together. Claire, the little-middle child, commented on the inconsistency of my texturing. I told her that someone had said, "Consistency is the hobgoblin of small minds." She said, "What's a hobgoblin?" She had me stumped, so I had to look it up and "hobgoblin" means "a mischievous goblin" or a "bugaboo." She said that that didn't make much sense. I couldn't argue with her. But later I looked into the quote further and it turns out that the exact quote is "A foolish consistency is the hobgoblin of little minds, adored by little statesmen and philosophers and divines." So now it's clear. Who said it? Ralph "Where's Waldo" Emerson, who knew absolutely nothing about texturing walls.

One of my daughters, her name is withheld to protect the guilty, was recently talking to a friend on the phone, when it was time to leave the house. She continued her conversation as she got in the car and drove off. She didn't go far when the phone went dead. She quickly realized that she wasn't using her cell phone, but the cordless house phone. It reminds me of one time back in the 70's when I went through a bank drive-thru and kept the tube. When I got back to work, I realized that I still had the tube and had to take it back. Like father, like daughter. The only difference is that no one saw my daughter's mistake. The folks at the bank are still laughing at me.

Being a middle child is difficult. The oldest always got to do more things, the younger one was the "baby" and got more attention, so life didn't seem equitable to the little middle child. Claire was, for several years, known around our house as "It's Not Fair, Claire."

But, when talking to Claire, she mentioned that they had been to a movie. I asked how it was and she said it was a "renter." I didn't understand, but she explained that it was OK, but not worth the $17 movie admission charge, but would be OK for the $3 rental. I asked how many folks went to the movie for $17. It was just Claire and Gavin. The cost of a movie in North Dallas is now $8.50 per person. This made me think of the cost of a movie back in the 50's. I can remember 9 cents. Popcorn was a nickel and so was a cold drink. Parents could give their kids a quarter, drop them off at the "picture show" (we didn't have "movies" back then) let them have a coke and popcorn and get 6 cents back in change. And they would ask for the change. From 9 cents to $8.50 is an increase of 94 times. Wow.

What else has increased so dramatically in the last 50 years? Ice cream cones used to be a nickel and they are now about $1.75. That's 35 times as much. A package of chewing gum used to be nickel and now it's about 95 cents, so that's an increase of 19 times. I'm guessing that cars are about 8 times as expensive as they were in the 50's. Houses about 10 times as expensive. I think we should have bought a "picture show" in the 50's and just held on.

A few weekends ago, we had our annual (men only) family deer hunt. No one in the family hunts deer anymore, but we enjoy the great outdoors and also get to watch a lot of football games without the normal interruption of Honey Do's and Honey Don'ts. While no one wants to shoot Bambi, there is a strong desire to shoot wild hogs. There are a couple of reasons for this. One, the hogs do a lot of damage to crops and fields. Two, there's something kind of exciting about trying to kill something that is so wild and ugly and mean. Three, some people actually cook and eat the hogs, but it's an awful lot of trouble and very messy and doing so deprives the buzzards of a great meal.

So anyway, my two sons-in-law and brothers-in-law and nephew-in-law killed a couple of wild hogs. Gavin, my North Dallas area son-in-law wanted to share this moment (the hog killin) with his four-year-old son, my grandson, Jack. So, he took a picture of the hog with his Blackberry, emailed it to Jack and then called him to tell him to go look at the email. All of this was done in one minute from the middle of a pasture in the middle of the country near Pidcoke, Texas. Jack wanted his Dad to bring the hog home, but that didn't work out. Not sure what Jack would have done with a dead hog, probably jumped up and down on him. His mother would also have done a lot of jumping up and down, but on Jack's father.

Anyway, we kind of take this amazing technology for granted, but can you imagine 20 years ago, if someone had told you that you would be able to take a picture in the middle of a field in the middle of nowhere and instantly send it through the air to someone hundreds of miles away and then call them and talk about it? Well, we would have thought that they were crazy. The next thing, they would have told us that our cars would talk to us and tell us when and where to turn to get to an unknown location. Crazy people!

Grandchildren
(SERIOUSNESS ALERT)

Our first grandchild was born in February, 2001. It was a traumatic experience and I wrote about it in my column, as follows:

We (or at least I) tend to get lost in our own worlds sometimes. I've been like that for the last few weeks.

Vicki and I are brand new, first time grandparents. (I will now pause while all of you say to yourselves, "Surely he's too young to be a grandfather!" Are you finished?) I'm not really too young, I just look too young. (You're not buying that either, are you?) Well, at least I feel too young. My daughter Claire (the mother of our grandchild) asked a few months ago what I wanted to be called by my soon-to-be-arriving granddaughter. After some thought, I decided on "Uncle Jack." No one's buying that either.

Our granddaughter, Caroline Elizabeth, was born on February 23rd at about 9 weeks early. She tipped the scales at 2 pounds, 15 ounces and then soon dropped to 2 pounds, 7 ounces. Like all "preemies" she has had a myriad of problems but is hanging in there as this is written. The first time we saw her we could hardly see her, she had so many tubes, wires and leads and monitors attached to her. Gradually they are being removed.

The night before Caroline was born, my wife, Vicki, called Claire to see how she was doing and discovered that she was in severe pain which earlier in the week was thought to be indigestion. After a discussion between Vicki and our son-in-law it was decided to take Claire to the emergency room. (Gavin is a good son-in-law. He obeys his mother-in-law.) Claire was admitted to the hospital and a battery of tests was begun. At about 3:30 in the morning we got a call saying that the doctor thought it was probably a gall bladder problem and that her gall bladder would have to be removed the next day. Gavin said he would call us back when the surgery was scheduled.

We got a call at about 9:00 the next morning saying that the doctors now said it wasn't a gall bladder problem, but that Claire had a rare problem known as HELLP Syndrome, which was potentially fatal and that the only way to save the mother's life was to "deliver the baby." We headed for Dallas. Surgery would be performed as soon as possible. Claire went in for surgery and about 11:30 our oldest daughter reported to us on our car phone that the surgery was over and that Mother and Daughter were doing "as well as could be expected." HELLP (Hemolysis, Elevated Liver enzymes, Low Platelets) syndrome is very unusual in that the only cure is removing the baby, but it is basically an instant cure. The mother immediately begins to recover, and Claire did. Caroline, on the other hand, has had good days and bad days and each day is an adventure.

There are several things that I have learned. First, modern medical practitioners can be miracle workers. Secondly, prayer works. We had and have hundreds of friends, family and total strangers praying for Caroline. Was it the doctors and nurses or divine providence? A combination of both? God only knows. He really does.

Caroline is now 12 years old and an exceptional human and granddaughter.

(END SERIOUSNESS ALERT)

Speaking of children, my 4-year-old grandson, Jack, recently went to his first high school football game. Catholics have first communion and confirmation. Jews have a bar mitzvah for their young men. Southern Protestants take their boys to a high school football game as a "right of passage." (Do liberal Democrats [pardon the redundancy] have a "left of passage?") Anyway, my son-in-law, Gavin took Jack to his first high school game because an old college friend was the coach. When Jack got home, his mother asked him how it was, and Jack said that it pretty cool except for the orange-haired lady who didn't like the team's socks. This was confusing. Claire asked him what was wrong with the socks and Jack said that there was nothing wrong with the socks; they were a nice red and white. Claire asked what the orange-haired lady said. Jack said that she was mad and kept yelling "You Sock!" Well, apparently the orange-haired lady was mad at the referee. Some things are best unexplained. Maybe this was the "wrong of passage." Wonder what the referee's socks looked like?

Speaking of sports, I have another great tip for you entrepreneurs out there. My oldest grandson, Jack, is a budding athletic star. He could hit the ball in T-Ball and run and slide into first and then get up and run and slide into second and then run and slide into third and then run and slide into home. A homerun with four slides has to be a record. But back to the entrepreneurial thing (I like to spell that word). Jack got his T-Ball trophy this year and slept with it for a few nights. (I didn't say he had perfect judgment, just that he is a great little athlete.) Anyway, it seems to me that sleeping with a sharp-pointed metal trophy couldn't be too comfortable. Therefore, someone needs to produce Plush-Toy-Trophies, suitable for sleeping companionship. You're welcome.

Vicki and I have 5 grandchildren, 4 boys and one girl. There are lots of reasons why granddaughters are special, just like grandsons. Granddaughters are cute and sweet and smart (mine is, of course, cuter and smarter and sweeter than others) and fun to talk to. But another reason that granddaughters are really great is...Girl Scout cookies. If a stranger comes to your door selling Girl Scout cookies, you might buy a box or two, but if your granddaughter is selling Girl Scout cookies you need to buy at least ten. Ten boxes of GS cookies are ten times better than one box. And also when you buy food for a good cause, it's not fattening. If no one else has already claimed that proposition...I'll call it Smith's Law Of Benevolent Shopping or SLOBS for short. Eat more Girl Scout cookies, slobs. It's for a good cause.

My oldest Austin grandson, John Matthew, who is six years old, was stacking and counting the coins that he found in his plastic Easter eggs. I asked him what he was going to do with his money and he looked up and said, "Tax-Free Muni's." After I quit laughing, I learned that it was a family joke, and that he didn't come up with it himself.

My Austin grandkids were eating out and the food was a little slow in coming. One of the four-year-old twins, Luke, asked his Mom a good question. "Why are they called waiters, when we're the ones waiting?" Good question, Luke. I can see law school in your future.

Another of my Austin grandsons has secured a place on Art Linkletter's "Kids Say the Darndest Things" TV show, should he or it be revived. (If you've never heard of Art Linkletter, ask your parents or some other old dude or dudette.) Anyway, John Matthew commented on his Mother's new shirt. He said, " I like that shirt. It makes you look prettier than you really are." Was that a compliment?

CHAPTER EIGHT

The
Good Old Days

We old folks like to talk and remember the good old days. At least those of us who can still remember stuff, which pretty much leaves me out.

Is it "good old days" or "good ole days?" What is "ole?" Well, it means "bravo" in Spanish. It is "a chemical compound containing a 5-membered heterocyclic ring." (But you knew that.) It can also mean "old." So who cares? Either one is OK.

Sometimes I miss the good old (ole) days, but I'd hate to be without my computer, TV remote control, zip lock bags, cruise control, Teflon cooking utensils, Internet, cell phones and HD TV.

I wish we could have all of the modern conveniences and the more gentle lifestyles of the past. When I was a child, my folks left the car keys in the car all the time and never locked our house doors, even at night. Our schools had great teachers, very few administrators and mostly disciplined students. The federal or state government rarely made demands of our schools or our businesses. Kids played baseball without adult supervision. The neighbors knew their neighbors and even knew and played with the roaming neighbor's dogs. Governments lived within their means. (Younger readers might not believe this, but it really happened.)

Of course, there were a lot of bad things that happened also, but generally I'd trade for what is happening today.

As they say, if the music is too loud, you're too old. That's me in a nutshell.

A friend recently mentioned something about something being kept in a cigar box. I hadn't thought of cigar boxes in a long time. I'll bet that most young people have never seen a cigar box, but I do remember that a lot of things were kept in them in the good old days of the last century. But I wonder…where did we get all of those cigar boxes? My father didn't smoke cigars (my mother didn't either), and yet we always seemed to have colorful cigar boxes around to keep stuff in. Today we have plastic storage boxes of all sizes and shapes, but they don't have the charm of a cigar box. Did cigar boxes smell like cigars?
I don't remember that.

Other things that have changed since my childhood are national magazines. In the old days, it seems, there were only three really big national magazines. *Life, Look* and *The Saturday Evening Post*. Now there is one magazine for every ten people. If you're a left-handed, redheaded stamp collector from Wyoming, there's a magazine just for you. Times have changed and the focus has changed. Looking at magazine titles and the concepts that they represent, you can see a progression of thought. We have gone from *Life* (everybody and most everything) to *People* (just the human beings) to *Us* (a smaller group of human beings) to *Self* (just you or just me). For the *Life* of me, I can't figure out why *People*, like *Us*, have become so *Self* centered.

We found an old blanket in storage and couldn't decide what to do with it. Vicki looked for washing instructions and it said to "Dry on Parallel Lines." That's a real old blanket. Today's young folks would think that "parallel lines" was some kind of math problem (or drug problem). When I was a kid, we had a clothesline in our back yard, but we weren't so highfalutin that we had "parallel" lines. If you ask a kid today what a "clothesline" is, they would probably say "Gap" or "Tommy Hilfiger."

Speaking of the "good-ole-days" and the name Jack reminds me of Cracker Jacks. Cracker Jacks are still around and I guess they still have prizes in them. I sing in a church choir and our choir director is a completely normal choir director. He's weird. One evening at practice he mentioned Cracker Jack. Everyone in the choir agreed that it was Cracker "Jacks," in the plural. He insisted that he was right and the next week he brought a Cracker Jack box. Just one Jack. I was amazed. I can't imagine singing, "buy me some peanuts and cracker jack." But we don't sing that in church anyway. At least not yet. The weird one could suggest it, however.

Those of you who are close to my age (about half the age of dirt) will know who Norma Jeane Baker and Marion Morrison are. For you younger folks, they would be Marilyn Monroe and John Wayne. (Would John Wayne have made it if he had stuck with Marion?) In the "good ole days" actors changed their names to names that were thought to be more appealing and easier to remember. Like most everything else, things have changed. At the opening credits of TV shows, they flash the names of the actors rather quickly and it's difficult to read them sometimes. But here are the names of actors on NYPD Blue: Mark-Paul Gosselaar, Bill Brochturp, Jaqueline Obradors, Gordon Clapp and Garcelle Beauvais-Nilon. Folks on various CSI's include: Marg Helgenberger, Paul Guilfoyle, Eric Szmanda and Khandi Alexander. (If the latter two should marry, the new bride would be Khandi Szmanda. Easy for you to say.) The good old days had some good old ideas.

In the good old days, each year a nice person from the phone company would drop by your home and give you a new phone book for each phone that you had and ask if you needed more. Now, once a year, some unseen person throws a phone book in a plastic bag into my front yard, perhaps behind a hedge. It's not exactly a "drive-by" crime, but it's close. We have three phones and get one phone book thrown in our yard. If you want more phone books, what do you do? I don't know. I haven't found the phone company customer service office. I haven't looked either, because I don't think there is one. Of course it's only old people who use or care about a phone book. Young folks don't need one because cell phone numbers aren't in there anyway.

I still can't get used to seeing police cars for school districts. Again, in the good old days, the teacher would handle discipline problems and if she needed help, she'd send the bad kid to the principal's office where he would be "taken care of." I never saw a real policeperson at my school, much less a school cop. School cops didn't exist because they weren't needed. Do we have armed hall monitors these days? I can't think of anywhere I go on a normal day where the presence of policepersons is required. Not at work, not at restaurants, not at home. Are schools that dangerous? What do school cops do? Do they bust 3rd graders for chewing gum? Do the cafeterias have do-nuts?

TV HAS CHANGED SINCE ITS GOOD OLD DAYS. IT'S GONE FROM BLACK AND WHITE TO COLOR TO OFF COLOR.

When I was young (way back in the last century) doctors wore dress shirts and ties, under their starched white examination coats. (When I was young, I didn't know a female doctor, so I don't remember what they wore.) Now many doctors and their staff members wear scrubs. Scrubs are kind of like pajamas, but less interesting. At least when they get up in the morning, they don't have to worry about what they're going to wear today. I bet doctors, in their pajamas all day, are getting more hours of sleep. Maybe that's why you have to wait in the waiting room, the docs are taking a nap. I think it would be nice to find a doctor that has a "no-waiting room" and is dressed for success. On the other hand, they may make you wait in the doctor's office so you will time to read *The Wacoan*.

I was told that if you eat the exact same meal everyday you should lose weight. Maybe because it gets so boring that you quit eating much. I worked at the state capitol (leading guided tours) while in college and ate the exact same meal every day. A ham sandwich, Fritos and a coke. The very small food place in the capitol basement had a limited fare and was managed by the Blind Commission. The cashier was a very nice older blind lady. When you gave her a bill, you had to tell her if it was a $1 a $5 or a $10. (I don't think I ever had a $20.) Think that could happen today? Today when you give someone a $20 bill, they use a marker to see if it's real or counterfeit. Ah, the good old days.

CHAPTER NINE

English
And Words

As previously mentioned, my Dad was a stickler for proper English and grammar. There were few meals (some younger readers might not understand the concept of the whole family sitting down at a table and eating meals together) that were finished without my brother or I (just kidding) being corrected for saying things like "my brother and I." It seemed repetitive and unnecessary at the time, but I pretty much appreciate it today.

The English language is strange. It's good to be "an interesting person" but not so good to be "a person of interest."

I heard someone say that so-and-so was "Three sheets to the wind." That usually means "over-served" or in pig latin (igpay atinlay)...unkdray. What does "three sheets to the wind" mean? I looked it up. It has to do with the sails on a sailboat. A "sheet" is a chain or a rope that is attached to the lower corner of a sail to control it. On a sailboat with three sails, if the "sheets" are loosened the ship will run wild with sails flapping. So if a sailor was so unkdray that he couldn't navigate the boat, he was said to be "three sheets to the wind". Maybe today, a drunk runs wild with jaws flapping instead of sails.

Another saying I heard said recently was "to the victor goes the spoils." Who wants to win a bunch of spoiled stuff? I looked it up.

Originally it was "to the victor goes the spoils of war" and was a term used as far back as 1300. It meant "valuable goods" and came from the Latin (not pig latin...try to keep up.) word spolium meaning animal hide. And of course, animal hide is different than hiding animals...instead of "hide and seek" it was seeking hides. So basically if you win the contest, you get the animal hides, if you really wanted them, which you probably didn't.

Wonder why "phonetic" isn't spelled with an "F"?

When will we quit calling the "glove box" a "glove box?" (Maybe at the same time we quit "rolling up car windows" and "dialing" phones.) When did you last put gloves in the glove box? Maybe it should be called "the most junk, not including gloves, we can cram in there and still close the door" compartment.

I heard someone say recently that something happened in "one fell swoop." What in the world is "one fell swoop?" Well, I tried to look it up. One of the definitions of "fell" is: fierce, cruel, terrible. Who knew? So, what's a "swoop?" The dictionary says a "swoop," as a noun, would mean the "art of swooping." That's helpful. As a verb, "swoop" means "to move with a sweep." So, what's a "sweep"? Probably, in this case, a "sweeping motion." So, probably the best use of the phrase "one fell swoop" would be when a hawk spotted a field mouse down below and flew down (in a fierce sweeping motion) and captured the dirty rat. It has come to mean, in general terms, "all at once" or "in one continued motion." So there you are, the answer...in one fell swoop. So, who first used this awkward phrase? Blame it on Shakespeare. He used it in Macbeth, Act 1, Scene 3 as Macduff learned that his whole family had been murdered "in one fell swoop," which in 1605 in England was spelled "fwoope." If they couldn't spell any better than that, it's no wonder we kicked their behinds in the Revolutionary War.

Speaking of out-of-date phrases, when was the last time you heard a female excuse herself to go "powder her nose?" Did the use of cocaine make this phrase unacceptable? And why was just the nose so in need of powder? What about cheeks, foreheads, chins?

Did you know that the "C" in Rap Music is silent?

I heard someone say recently that something should be done "posthaste." That's an odd word. The dictionary says it means "with all possible speed." But if you look up the word "post" there are many definitions including the one that means "after," as in postgraduate or postdate. So wouldn't posthaste mean "after" haste, which wouldn't be too fast at all? You're right. Who cares?

I'd bet that there's at least one word in the English language (press 2) that has all of the vowels in order...and I'm not being facetious.

Speaking of vowels, they say to put the "I" before the "E" except after C. That's weird.

Still speaking of English (press 2), a lady asked the operator for the phone number of a person named "Caseway." The operator asked her to spell it and so she said, "OK. That's C as in cave. A as in aye. S as in sea. E as in eye. W as in why. A as in are. Y as in you." The supervisor couldn't help either.

The Washington Post each year has a contest in which it asks readers to submit new definitions for existing words. Some of my favorites this year were: Coffee (n.) a person who is coughed upon...Flabbergasted (adj.) appalled over how much weight you have gained...Lymph (v.) to walk with a lisp...Balderdash (n.) a rapidly receding hairline.

I decided to open the dictionary at random, point to a word and see if it would lend itself to a new definition. I first pointed to "forsake." So... Forsake (n.) a person who favors alcoholic beverages from Japan. I tried again and pointed to "mesmerize." So...Mesmerize (n.) eyes that look like mesmer. Obviously, it doesn't always work.

I ran across the phrase "fast asleep" the other day. It's a curious term. It doesn't mean to fall asleep quickly, but rather to be in a "sound" or "deep" sleep. I don't think that I'm often fast asleep, but I frequently seem to be "slow awake." Sometimes I think that the "senior moment" concept stretches into a senior week or senior month.

You frequently hear people saying, "I could care less!" Of course if they "could care less," that means that they do care some. What they mean to say is "I couldn't care less!" Wonder how that opposite-of-what-I mean expression got started?

One of the things I notice about getting old is that I can't spend nearly as much time doing yard work as I used to. This is not necessarily a bad thing, but when it's really hot, I can only spend about 15 minutes or so pulling weeds or whatever before I feel a need to sit down in the shade and rest for a bit. I seem to become "light-headed". I was thinking about this and wondered if I were to sit in my recliner in the air conditioning watching a mindless TV show (the kind that I like) for an extended period of time, would I become "heavy-headed?" If you do feel heavy-headed, what do you do? Yard work?

If you found that you had way too much duffel, do you think you could find some kind of bag to put it in?

I recently heard someone say that someone else was "in the catbird seat." What's a catbird and where is his seat? Well, I looked it up. A catbird is the North American Thrush or the Dumetella Carolinensis. (You don't know if I made that up or not.) It's called a "catbird" because its cry somewhat resembles the mew of a cat. Being in the "catbird seat" means "sitting pretty." I personally have neither sat pretty, nor been in the catbird's seat. The phrase was popularized by Red Barber (not a Native-American hair stylist, but a baseball announcer) who worked for the Brooklyn Dodgers who now play in Los Angeles where there may or may not be a catbird.

I heard someone say that someone else was "wreaking havoc" on something. It's kind of a strange phrase. I have a pretty good idea what "havoc" is (my dictionary says "wide spread destruction") but what exactly is "wreak" and why is havoc the only thing we ever seem to wreak? Well, I'm glad you asked. "Wreak" according to the very same dictionary, is basically "to bring about." So you could also "wreak" peace and love if you wanted to, but it probably wouldn't work. It might cause too much havoc.

I saw an ad on TV for a Lazy Susan. I wonder where it got the name. It could have been a Lazy Mary, or Dorothy or Rose Mary or Patricia or Lazy Liz. What did Susan do so bad?

I read recently where someone was accused of being "ruthless." I wondered where that term originated. "Ruthless," the dictionary says, means, "having no ruth" or "merciless or cruel." "Ruth" is defined as "compassion for the misery of another." I wondered if one can be "ruthful?" Yes, one can. The dictionary says that "ruthful" means "full of ruth" or "full of sorrow." Are you sorrowful that I brought this up? I'm all ruthful about it.

WHAT IF YOU LOOKED UP THE WORD "CONSPIRACY" IN THE DICTIONARY AND IT WASN'T THERE?

I read recently where someone said something, "in no uncertain terms." I wonder why we use this double negative? Why don't we just say things in "certain terms?"

Speaking of dictionaries, I heard that there is a new Thesaurus in bookstores. Critics have described it is as Inferior, Deficient, Defective, Tainted, Below-Par.

Let's golf. Why do some folks use golf as a verb? As in... "Do you golf?" You don't hear anyone asking, "Do you football? Do you baseball? Do you track? No, we play baseball, football...run track and we also play golf. So cut it out.

One never knows what will create interest. Usually nothing in this column does, but every now and then a major issue arises. I wrote last month that the word "golf" is a noun and that people should quit using it as a verb. You don't golf...you play golf. This created a tremendous amount of controversy (that means that three people commented). I decided to be sure that I was correct so I called Merriam Webster. First I told him that Merriam was an awfully strange name for an old man. He said his name wasn't Merriam, but Noah. I don't know if he was telling the truth or not, after all, he's been dead for 167 years. Anyway, goofy name or not, he declared that "golf" is definitely a noun, just as he said it was in his big book. So there.

I heard one of the Senators from California (I get them mixed up) say that we needed to increase the "securitization" in Iraq. Why don't we just increase the "security" in Iraq? I heard another politician say that we need to "securitize" something. Why not just "secure" it. Why do government people like to make up unnecessary words? Maybe it's a "wordization" movement.

Speaking of words... we have "yesterday" and "yesteryear," but not "yesterweek" or "yestermonth." Why not? A week can be just as "yester" as a day. And why does "yesterday" mean the day before and "yesteryear" mean many years ago?

Marlin
Meets Europe

A few years ago, Vicki and I had the wonderful opportunity to travel with a group of 16 Central Texans and 22 other folks from around the USofA on an 11-day tour to London, Paris, Rome and home.

It's a little different in Europe than in Falls County. For one thing, most all of those folks talk funny. Below is an article that I wrote after our trip. There is one factual error that Vicki was quick to point out after the article was printed. See if you can discover it. The answer will be at the end of the article. If you can, you get points. Point redemption is difficult, but you might try calling your congressperson. The article had a picture of me standing beside a Smart Car in one of those cities that we visited.

The car in the picture is called a Smart car. I think it's made by Mercedes and it's the hottest vehicle in Europe. It's the size of a small golf cart and looks like somebody stole the backseat and rest of the car. I was told that the price and the gas mileage were not exceptional, but you can park them anywhere. They pull into a parking spot sideways, frontways or backways. The car is the same length and width. While in Europe for nine days we saw two pickup trucks, no 18-wheelers and one SUV (an older model Jeep Cherokee). A Smart car would make it on I-35 for about three minutes before being blown off the road by an 18-wheeler and it wouldn't be found in the weeds until winter.

Not only does Europe have no pickups they also have no ice and no air conditioning and no butter and no salt. They actually have them, but they don't want you to use them. They save ice and a/c and salt like we try to save time and money.

They don't save money. Cokes were sometimes $6. Ice cream cones could be $5. The average full meal deal at a restaurant was $30 and up, which may have included wine, but not a coke or ice or butter or salt or air conditioning. Our delightful London tour guide said he was buying a 600 square foot "flat" for $280,000. Apartments in England are called "flats" because if you buy one you will be "flat" broke.

The hotels actually do have air conditioning; they just don't turn it on. We were told it wasn't hot enough. We later found out that they don't turn on the a/c until June 1st. They run their air conditioning not by the thermostat, but by the calendar.

Europeans have a restaurant on every corner and people eat constantly. They eat a lot of cheese and bread and yet you have to search for an overweight native. If you see an overweight person the odds are it's a tourist. I don't know exactly why, but I think it's the amount of walking that they do. I ate like a pig for 10 days and lost 5 pounds. We walked from 5 to 10 miles a day. Seriously. The food was mostly good. I frequently didn't know what I was eating, but it was OK. I think I ate rabbit and duck and maybe pigeon or horse at the same meal in Rome.

We rode the bullet train from London to Paris at 180 mph. It was remarkably smooth and you didn't realize how fast you were going until we paralleled a highway and zoomed past the cars like they were standing still. (Maybe they were standing still while someone stole their backseats and the rest of the car.)

We also used the subways in London and Paris extensively. It's amazing how quickly and efficiently they move hundreds of thousands of people every day. They don't have much of a subway system in Rome because every time they dig they discover more ancient ruins and have to stop. Blame the hysterical society.

I saw a political poster (in either Paris or Rome) urging folks to vote for the Communist Party. Isn't that a bit ironic? Communists want you to vote? I guess they have to get enough votes before they can do away with voting.

All three cities that we visited are "river cities" like Waco. The Thames (which they don't have a clue how to pronounce) in London, the

Seine (possibly named after people seining for minnows) in Paris, and the Tiber (named after Tiber) in Rome. They have done a much better job of developing their riverfronts than we have. But they had a couple of thousand-year head start on us. We'll catch up.

Roger Miller sang "Eng-guh-lun swings like a pendulum do. Bobbies on bicycles, two by two". If he had been grammatically correct, he would have written, "Eng-guh-lun swings like a pendulum does. The guys on bikes, must be the fuzz".

For all of the things that Europe doesn't have, they do have history. Everywhere. When you walk on the beautiful marble floor of the Pantheon in Rome, the exact same floor that people walked on 500 years before Christ, it makes you stop and think. I was thinking about whether I could get ice or butter or salt at supper.

In London I rode the Millennium Wheel (the world's largest Ferris wheel at 405 feet tall, more than one and a half times taller than the Alico building), saw where Winston Churchill lead WW II efforts (underground), toured the Tower of London (where beheading people was a major spectator sport), saw the Crown Jewels at Windsor Castle (the Queen was there at the time, but didn't come out to greet us as she was probably busy trying to find some ice and get the air conditioning going), toured Westminster Abby (where a whole lot of famous dead people are buried) and saw the changing of the guard at Buckingham Palace. I hope they don't ever try to fight a war in those uniforms.

In Paris, I went to the top of the Eiffel Tower, toured the Louvre, took a beautiful night boat trip down the Seine, drove around the Arch de Triumph, toured Notre-Dame Cathedral and attended the Rotary Club of Paris where the noon meal cost $64.51 American money. The Louvre is probably the world's most famous museum. It would take days or maybe weeks to see it all, but a couple of hours were more than enough for a clod like me. When you see one statue of a nude man or woman with an arm or nose broken off, you've seen them all. I had a feeling that the Great Masters' paintings were painted by number. They all looked alike to me. I never took art appreciation. Obviously.

In Rome we visited the Pantheon, the Vatican, including the Sistine Chapel (that Michelangelo could paint one heck of a ceiling), the Coliseum and the Forum. Some of our tour group got to see the Pope at a beatification ceremony. On the last night, our last stop was the famous Trevi Fountain. In the movie *Three Coins in the Fountain* I think the couple was all alone at the romantic fountain. In reality, there were a thousand tourists, 30 deep in front of it. You had to wait in line and muscle your way to get close enough to throw your coins (only two coins thrown with your right hand over your left shoulder). Parking in Rome was like parking in downtown Austin. Every parking space in the city, and many that weren't, was taken. If I win the lottery, I'm going to invest in a parking garage in Rome. There are no driving rules in Rome. The boldest has the right of way. With all of the tiny little wanta-be-cars, if you had a Suburban or Expedition you could be the absolute king of the road. (Roger Miller just keeps popping up.)

There wasn't a lot of security in evidence anywhere we went. There were three French soldiers walking around the grounds of the Eiffel Tower with weapons, but I think they were trying to find someone to whom they could surrender.

We didn't see or feel any anti-Americanism other than one brief episode in which a tour guide began to bad-mouth American healthcare. Someone asked him how long you had to wait for a hip or knee replacement in England and he said "two or three years." That pretty much ended the debate. Everyone else seemed to be very pleased to have us there spending our money.

Speaking of money, both English pounds and Euro dollars have $1 and $2 coins that are used a lot. The reason they are used a lot is that the smallest "bill" is a $5 bill. So if our government is really serious about using dollar coins, they need to do away with the dollar bill. It would work just fine.

P.S. Vicki said that in my recent random thoughts about our trip to Europe I wrote that we saw the Crown Jewels at Windsor Castle. She said that it would come as a big shock to the folks at the Tower of London to learn that they had lost their crown jewels. Picky, picky, picky. When you "see" the Crown Jewels you have to look quickly because you're on a moving indoor sidewalk, kind of like a treadmill. I waved as I went by.

CHAPTER ELEVEN

If
I Were King

At the end of my monthly column I have an "If I Were King" suggestion. Things I would do if I had the power. I once considered doing a little book or a comic strip type deal of IIWK things, but somebody already had the If I Were King web site, so I was discouraged. A former Waco friend of mine (former Wacoan, not former friend) was (or probably still is) a cartoonist. I enticed him (it's amazing what cash will do) to create some cartoons to match my thoughts. Some are included, just to add visual impact and the number of pages to the book.

Usually I finish writing my column and then spend a couple of days trying to think of something that really bugs me that I would correct if I were king. One month I just gave up and wrote: If I Were King, sometimes I'd take the month off.

PETA members have of late, recommended that college students drink beer rather than milk to save cows from the pain and embarrassment of milking and have also protested the treatment of fish at fishing tournaments. IF I WERE KING, PETA members would get a life...drop the

E... become PTA members and worry about how teachers and students are treated rather than cows and fish.

If I Were King:

Cats would come when you called them, and wouldn't if you didn't.

Anyone who put an obscene bumper sticker on his car would have two flat tires every morning until he took it off.

Anyone with visible tattoos and body piercings would be prohibited from winning the lottery. God only knows what they might do with a lot of money.

It would have to rain on at least half of the days that the TV Weather-Guessers predict it will.

Smoking would cause teenagers to have very serious pimple problems.

People with body odor would have an inordinate fear of elevators.

If I Were King:

The person who came up with the term "significant other" would be barred from speaking or writing in English (if indeed he or she ever did).

All terrorists would be put in a large stadium where they would fight each other until only one remained alive. He would move to New Zealand and become a shepherd.

There would never be ice on a Texas road. We just can't hack it.

People who send unsolicited emails about get-rich-quick schemes, free credit cards, free trips, free stock tips, cheap insurance and cheap mortgage rates would suffer a constant "error" message on their computer and on their foreheads.

Television sitcom writers could think of funny things to write about that we could watch with our children or parents or grandparents without being embarrassed.

Eating chicken fried steaks, french fries and Texas toast, all with cream gravy, would cure cancer, obesity and the common cold.

If I Were King:

In most training situations, trainees are required to show that they have perfected their knowledge and skills to the other trainees prior to going out into the general public to exhibit their abilities. If I were king, this rule would be mandatory for suicide bombers.

It would be OK for "real men" to admit that they enjoy HGTV and The Antique Road Show.

Doctors, or maybe nurses, would decide how long patients stay in the hospital. Insurance companies would learn about it later.

The amount of calories required to chew food would equal the amount of calories in the food being chewed.

Those who send spam via email, would have to eat spam every meal until they quit sending it. Their spam meals would be called e-meals.

IF I WERE KING, I would have more time to get on the Atkins or South Beach diet. Right now my plate is just too full.

The Nobel Prizes would be much more practical. For instance, this year's Nobel Prize for Science would have been shared by the inventors of the TV Remote Control and the Zip Lock Bag.

Iran would do the world a favor by giving up their quest for nuclear weapons and instead concentrate on a solution for potholes.

Birds wouldn't get flu, cows wouldn't get mad and talk of pandemics would be academic.

Varmints who visit your garden would only eat weeds.

Anyone who even thought about hijacking or blowing up an airplane would have to wait in the airport security check line until starvation doth him part.

If I Were King:

Baseball would be played in the summer, football in the fall and basketball in the winter. Soccer and hockey could be played anytime, because nobody really cares.

Michael Savage would challenge Al Sharpton to a dual and they would both win.

There would be more vegetarians in Texas. They would never discuss their food decision in public but they would leave more meat for me.

BRITNEY, PARIS, LINDSEY AND ALL OF THE KARDASHINS WOULD JOIN A CONVENT AND TAKE A VOW OF SILENCE.

Arsonists would be consumed by their work.

If I Were King:

The candidates in presidential debates would be hooked up to lie detectors and the moderators would be hooked up to bias detectors. After about 30 minutes of silence, we could watch I Love Lucy reruns.

Grandparents wouldn't constantly brag about their grandchildren unless their grandchildren were as good looking, smart and sweet as mine are, which would be virtually impossible.

Congresspersons who vote for really dumb ideas like ethanol, would have to dress like NASCAR drivers, so we could see who their corporate sponsors are.

Since Congress is unwilling to take steps to make our country more energy independent, gasoline prices would be correlated to the approval rating of Congress, which now stands at about 9 percent. Nine percent of $4 would be 36 cents which is what gas would cost until they got their act together, which will probably be never.

There would be at least one day a year when political candidates could spend the day asking potentially embarrassing personal questions to members of the news media.

If I Were King:

People wouldn't worry so much about what other people think, because they don't seem to do it very often.

Scientists would quit worrying about Global Warming and study something serious like why black olives come in cans and green olives come in jars.

"Tax Returns" would. And "Tax Audits" wouldn't.

There would be no more congressional hearings shown or television, ever. Instead, the networks would cover clown conventions, which are more serious and meaningful.

There would be a requirement that TV shows be at least as good as the commercials.

Charlie Sheen and Lindsay Lohan would marry each other and disappear together, forever.

Today's schools would have less administrators, more empowered teachers, disciplined students and concerned parents. Oh well, it doesn't hurt to dream.

If I Were King:

The temperature would not be allowed to be a 100 degrees or higher for more than three times a year, & one of them would have to be in February.

Scientist would be as successful at creating smart people as they are at creating smart phones.

Prudes would take over all network and cable television production.

Time would still be a great healer, but it would become a whole lot better beautician.